THE COMMON TATER:

MUSINGS OF AN EASTERN KENTUCKY NEWSPAPER COLUMNIST

By

John Sparks

Copyright 2016, 2017, 2018 by John Sparks. All rights reserved. Fair use granted for quotation of brief passages in reviews.

Also by John Sparks:

The Roots of Appalachian Christianity: the Life and Legacy of Elder Shubal Stearns (University Press of Kentucky, 2001, 2005).

Raccoon John Smith: Frontier Kentucky's Most Famous Preacher (University Press of Kentucky, 2005).

On Edge (Blue Cubicle Press, 2007).

The Last Dance of Gus Finley: a Tale of Eastern Kentucky Justice (Old Seventy Creek Press, 2009).

Kentucky's Most Hated Man: Charles Chilton Moore and the Bluegrass Blade (Wind Publications, 2009).

Waiting for God, O. T.: the Tom Harman Stories, Volume One (KYStory, 2016).

Family Wreath: the Tom Harman Stories, Volume Two (KYStory, 2016).

CONTENTS:

Welcome to the Tater Patch 11

My Career as a Bootlegger 15

Blow George 20

Elisha's Bears 25

The Reign of King Mob 29

Standup Guy 34

A Pocketful of Father's Day 39

The Sacrifice of Lucinda Mills 43

Just My Ten Cents' Worth 47

Hospital Drama 51

The Renaissance Men 55

Bearing Arms in Christian America, Part 1 60

Bearing Arms in Christian America, Part 2 64

Apocalypse Now! 69

Grandma and the Second Amendment 73

Quotation Remarks 77

Blackguardin' 81

The "A" Word 86

Pulpit Politics, Part 1 90

Pulpit Politics, Part 2 94

Squirrel & Muslims—or, AyMAYun? 98

Apple Days, Associations, & Yellow Jackets 103

The Rubaiyat of Joe & Kelly 107

The Gospel Fiddler 111

Halloween, Part 1: Corn Night 115

Halloween, Part 2: Haints 119

Shoutin' on the Hills of Glory 123

The Shoulders of Giants 127

If You Don't Talk About It, Part 1 132

If You Don't Talk About It, Part 2 136

Introducing Chuck Q. Farley 140

Early Times & Toenails 144

A Modest Proposal 149

The Days Were Accomplished 153

New Year's Cabbage 157

Im-taterment 161

Hear the Royal Proclamation 166

Pastoring, Politics, & Peanuts 170

Fake News & the Fillmore Bathtub 174

Groundhogs, Germans, & Grandfathers 179

That Old Time Religion 183

When Love Conquered All… or at Least Something 188

My Baptism Under Fire 192

Fan Mail 196

Bitter Twitter & Cruel Duels 200

In Defense of Ben 205

Another Modest Proposal 209

Lions, Lambs, & Lovin' 213

My God! 217

The Evolution of Friendship 222

Naturalized 226

The Kentucky Terrorist 231

FOREWORD: AN INTRODUCTION TO **SOLANUM TUBEROSUM**

In the spring of 2016, arguably the craziest, most hysterical period of recent years in American politics, Kathy Prater, the editor of a small eastern Kentucky family of newspapers known as Around Town, Inc., approached me about writing a weekly column for her Big Sandy Valley publications: Around Paintsville, Around Prestonsburg, and Around Louisa. At first I wondered why. I've been writing for some years now, and after one award from Morehead State University and another from the Kentucky Historical Society I guess I've built myself a little bitty reputation for it, deserved or not. But even so, the three non-fiction volumes springing from memories of my time two and three decades ago as a minister of religion are admittedly sort of dry as a matter of course, and my fiction, coming as it does largely from my equally longtime background as a hospital worker, is at best a mostly sardonic response to some very tragic situations. Not much fodder there for anyone looking for either tales of the Good Old Days through rose-colored glasses, or straight, hard-line conservative opinions reassuring readers of the truth of their already-established religious and political prejudices—in other words, the very essence of most Southern country newspaper columns.

    Maybe Kathy already had all the conservatism she could publish, perhaps even all she could handle, and was looking for a balance of some sort and requested my services. That might not be an entirely fair characterization, though. I don't consider myself a liberal or conservative either one, really, though the pejorative "libtard" sounds so unutterably stupid to me that anyone using it tempts me to classify myself as liberal. Truth told, I've been on both sides of a good many political, religious, and social questions at different times over the years, and I've come to enjoy poking fun at extremists on either fringe of an issue—more often than not, because I've been there at one time or another myself. That seems to be a constant source of confusion to my good buddy and inspiration, Chuck Q. Farley, though not so much so for his lovely wife, Polly Esther. But as to the other fundamental Southern newspaper column topic, Memories of the Past, as an historian I know that the Good Old Days weren't always or altogether good. I'm more inclined to agree with William Faulkner that the past isn't really dead; it's not even past. Again, not a fashionable attitude at all. Yet, for all that I'm completely out of step with current eastern Kentucky journalistic styles, Kathy and I tried the experiment of the column—and somehow, it seemed to work and even thrive. "The Common Tater" (and if you don't get the pun, for God's sake don't make me explain it; just check out the first essay) was born. And lived for about a year, which was as long as Around Town, Inc., stayed in business. The idea of a free local newspaper financed entirely by advertisements was laudable, but apparently not practical for an extended period of time in this part of the country.

In reading over these columns a year or so after their first publication, it strikes me as noteworthy that they still seem to be so germane. The dust has cleared just a little from 2016, but politics is still as crazy, and truth told, popular religion ain't all that far behind it (and I emphasize *popular,* which young people nationwide, even if perhaps not so much yet around here locally, seem to be abandoning in droves). Both are still mostly about images rather than issues, and if there's one thing I absolutely cannot abide, it's a preacher or any other sort of agitator with an agenda who whips up his (or her) hearers like cheerleaders at a pep rally into a frenzy over some nonsensical issue such as the goldsmiths and silversmiths of Ephesus did all the way back in Acts 19. Dang, what a run-on sentence that was; maybe I *can* still preach. Let him (or her) that readeth, understand. But anyway: things being as they are, maybe there's still a place in eastern Kentucky thought for these snippets of opinion, and therefore I offer them once again, here now.

Special thanks to Bob Abrams and Kathy Prater, formerly of Around Town, Inc., for the pulpit from which these little discourses were originally delivered, and to all the folks who gave me compliments on their content back in the day. I hope you enjoy seeing them again—and maybe do a double-take over a few, to boot. So here goes...

WELCOME TO THE TATER PATCH

Good day. My name's John, but for any and all practical purposes here within the sheets of *Around Paintsville* you may refer to me simply as the Common Tater. I've always been interested in reading and keeping up with newspaper columnists of the Kentucky variety, the favorites of my youth being Allen Trout and Joe Creason of the Louisville *Courier-Journal*—both of whom, incidentally, were themselves inspired by Henry Arrowood, a Johnson County writer who made good in the same periodical. I doubt that I'll ever attain the accomplishments of these three men, but it's still feels worth trying, and perhaps I can have a little fun along the way.

Why "The Common Tater"? Well, why not? When the idea of writing a column for

Around Paintsville was first suggested to me I thought about calling myself "The Mouth of Muddy Branch" in honor of the creek where I did most of my growing up, but another local writer whom I admire greatly sort of has the Muddy Branch franchise, and he's earned it entirely. Then I thought of "The Mouth of Greasy Creek" for the community where my wife—let's call her Sweet Tater—and I raised our two Tater Tots, but it's only right that Henry Arrowood should keep the laurels for the Boons Camp and Williamsport and Offutt communities. He had no less than three preacher brothers, and thus a lot of stories to tell. "The Mouth of Miller's Creek," one watercourse over from Greasy where I went a-courtin' one time—well, let's just say that one's Sweet Tater's purview. Then I considered "The Mouth of Burnt Cabin," the little branch just down the hill from where I presently reside, but after all the highway construction of the past century who really knows where or what Burnt Cabin Branch is anymore? In most people's minds nowadays it's "that little bitty creek across on the other side of Starfire Hill that runs along 321 and 1428," and it's been shifted so many times to accommodate asphalt there's no way to tell where its original bed was. Sort of like Town Branch in Lexington, or, for that matter, the Fleet River in London. You can't stop progress, though sometimes, at least in some aspects, you'd like to.

So I had to think of something else. Larry Webster's already got the copyright for "Red Dog," so unless I wanted to call myself "Red Horse" after the chewing tobacco "The Common Tater" was about all I had left. Still, as common a tater as I might be, I've come to realize that being a common tater isn't really so bad. The real harm in this world is done not so much by the common taters as it is by the specked taters. Everybody around here knows that specks signal the beginnings of rot on a tater, and the specked taters of this world are those who go through life complacently, simply trying to skate all the way, never speaking out in any form to improve the lot of their neighbors or make any real difference in the world around them and passing out of life as if they'd never even been *in* it in the first place. What's the point, if you can't make a positive difference? And that's the common tater's duty—to try to get the specked taters to scrape the specks off themselves, use their eyes (and yes, even a specked tater has them), and maybe—just maybe—do a little growing, even when the specked taters might accuse a common tater of throwing verbal fertilizer at them.

Again, good day and welcome. In this common tater patch I'll try to feature a little local history and political science along the way, though of a nonpartisan form and with the gentle reminder that, regardless of ideology, those who forget the past are condemned to repeat it; a bit of philosophy, albeit not of the long-haired complicated variety; a touch of religion, but not very much of the organized type because I've always believed that it's better for us to have questions that can never be answered than answers that can never be questioned; and throughout, hopefully, some amusement. I'd like to think that you could find something in this tater patch, sooner or later, that you'd want to dig up and take home with you. So it's past April already, and nearly Vine Day. Time to get this tater patch out.

MY CAREER AS A BOOTLEGGER

I doubt that I have to define this term for anybody locally yet, but I wonder if younger people can appreciate the word "bootlegger" like us older folk. Until perhaps the mid-1980s, bootlegging was a cottage industry locally. I watched my first-ever police liquor raid from the community schoolyard. Later I remember getting a crush on an older girl who "ran block" for one bootlegger, the main reason for my infatuation being that she could out-drive every lawman in the county who tried to catch her. In their day, bootleggers were both loved and maligned, but when we compare them with our modern illegal substance dealers, somehow they seem pretty tame.

But I do not mean to romanticize the "good old days." Yesteryear's old-time country physicians, so overwhelmed by cases of then-unknown depressive disorders and other mental conditions in addition to all the physical ailments that they had to treat, often gave out so-called "nerve tonic" indiscriminately simply to cope with their patient workloads. They look good compared to today's dealers too, but the old doctors' free-handedness with narcotics probably sowed the seeds of our modern addiction disaster more than the bootleggers ever did. Growing up, I can remember both neighbors and family members who'd never let a drop of whiskey pass their lips literally throw conniptions when they ran out of "nerve medicine" and couldn't get a refill quick enough. Sadly, the phrase "all things in moderation" has never had much of a fan club around these parts, but one memory of a wry old joke still remains as true as it ever was: any time a local-option election for liquor sales was held, preachers and bootleggers would always vote exactly the same way.

Which brings me to my own career as a bootlegger, which occurred not before but immediately after Paintsville "went wet." Things had just started to calm down after weeks of hot rhetoric from pulpit and paper, with both sermons and letters to the editor having prophesied drunks passed out on every corner and strip joints lining Main Street if the option passed. None of this occurred either then or after, of course, but at the time resentment locally between "wets" and "drys" was still mighty fresh and hot. And so about this time I met one of the latter, a preacher whom I'd known and worked with for several years, in a local market that had just begun to stock alcoholic beverages. I'll call him Brother Drye—no reflection on the quality of his sermons, but rather of his views on alcohol.

"Look at that," Brother Drye observed to me disgustedly as he pointed to the store's new liquor aisle. "Anybody who works here that calls himself a Christian should quit his job. If I could find one 'dry' store in town, I wouldn't be here either!"

"That's how the vote went," I replied, trying to be soothing. "Don't hold it against the workers."

"Well, it's not right," he retorted. "You know, I'd *love* to buy one of those little hip flasks to take into the pulpit with me and use it to preach about how bad liquor is. But I don't dare, because somebody'd see me and say I bought it for myself."

"Shoot, I'll go get one of those for you. Wait here," I offered, never asking how he knew they had hip flasks in stock unless he'd seen them. Maybe he'd heard it secondhand from a sinner.

He looked horrified. "Don't you know what people will say if they see you in that aisle?" he asked incredulously.

"Maybe 'Behold a gluttonous man, and a winebibber, a friend of publicans and sinners'?" I returned.

"They might!"

"And do you remember the fellow it was first said about?" I rejoined. (In case you don't have your concordance handy, it was Jesus, in Matthew 11:19 and Luke 7:34.)

"I know," he conceded with a sigh. "But they might say something else bad."

Anyway: I finally brazenly walked down the Aisle of Wickedness, bootlegged the hip flask for Brother Drye, paid for it myself because he was afraid to take it through the checkout line too, and then delivered it to him in the parking lot. Of course I let him have the flask at cost, taking no profit, but during the exchange he hunkered down so suspiciously next to his vehicle that any passing lawman who saw us would have had all the probable cause he needed to ask us what we were doing. Still, I do hope that Brother Drye got his money's worth from that shiny little bootleg trophy, no dry run-of-the-mill discourse but a fiery sermon with not a dry eye in the church house either. And although this incident doesn't compare with the trouble another preacher friend of mine got into years ago for buying Communion wine from a bootlegger (his congregation wanted him to send a sinner to get it instead), the old Common Tater still likes to rib Brother Drye about it whenever we see each other. After all, a merry heart doeth good like a medicine, but a broken spirit drieth the bones, and that's Bible too

(Proverbs 17:22). Of course, "all things in moderation" *isn't* a Bible phrase, but I still keep hoping it'll eventually catch on.

BLOW GEORGE

Blow george. There's no other term quite like it, but in eastern Kentucky, no other term that will do for its purpose. It means a person full of hot air, a braggart who's long on professing and short on possessing—what people in other regions of the United States might call a "gasbag," a "windbag," a "blowhard," a "blatherskite" (Mark Twain's personal favorite) or a "bull thrower," the first word of this latter term also lending itself to verbiage a little too strong for newsprint. "Blow george" could apply to almost anyone with a strong ego coupled with the gift of gab, be it a fisherman whose prize trout just keeps getting bigger and bigger with each recounting of its catch, or, say (just for the sake of argument), a newspaper columnist. So with so many other colorful, vivid words to choose from, how did the people of eastern Kentucky wind up with "blow george" as an expression?

The same way our conversation got itself flavored with so many other distinctive terms—the coal mines. The ventilation fans installed in the first mines ever opened in this area in the late nineteenth and early twentieth centuries were patterned after the design of the British mining engineer George Atkinson, himself a bit of an egoist who proudly titled his creation—you guessed it—the blow george. The apparatus was also known as the "windy king" in some areas, a great description itself for a braggart, but that term never caught on in Appalachia. A blow george could be operated by a steam engine connected to its crank by a piston, but in this area the enormous fans were far more often hand-cranked by very young miners (I'm talking ten- and eleven-year-olds here, since there were no Child Labor Laws at the time). A crew of six boys might spell each other out, by twos or threes, for ten or twelve hours a day, often five and a half or six days a week. And no doubt after a long hard shift of cranking a blow george to expel the rotten-egg-stinking black-powder smoke produced when coal was "shot," many an overworked child came to hate the fan, its distinctive title, and the hydrogen sulfide odor associated with its use, with an antipathy one had to "be there" to share. I can almost hear the term popping up practically automatically in the earliest coal camps, from the lips of boys and young men with backs and arms sore from a long day of thankless labor, listening to someone brag: "Good Lord, listen at that (expletive deleted) blow george go on and on!"

And yet when it comes to politics, eastern Kentuckians absolutely *adore* blow georges—not the mining apparatus, but the sort of people the term is used to describe. For many years before radio and television, political speeches and debates were first-class entertainment, and our most successful politicians were often also our most colorful. Perhaps with reality television, history is cycling back round. At least until after the Second World War, when a sizable bloc of voting veterans whose years of listening to the orders of blow-george military officers made for a modest change in political sentiment, throughout Kentucky and most of the rest of the South a candidate practically *had* to be a blow george to succeed. Though Carl Perkins pretty much qualified for the name too he didn't really count, because the fact he *was* a veteran got him elected the first time. He did most of his own blow-georging after that very first general election against Johnson County's own Howes Meade, though admittedly not without a lot of results both positive and negative over the years. The key, of course, was getting elected, and then keeping most of the people happy, or making them think that they were happy, at least a third or half the time, then getting ready for another blow-george campaign. Often, though, a blow george can go too far: in the 1930s Governor "Happy" Chandler's blow-george personal attack on Senator and later Vice President Alben Barkley earned Chandler the opprobrium of his entire political party, including President Roosevelt, and actually forced him out of politics for a brief while. And while this incident caused one of the strongest

Democrats I ever knew, my maternal grandfather, to vote Republican against Chandler every chance he got, Happy's blow-george style actually got him elected Governor again in the 1950s and even let him alter Kentucky's political landscape once more, in the 1960s—when Henry Ward beat him out for a Democratic nomination and he threw his support to Louie Nunn in retaliation, ushering in the era when West Virginia had Moore and Kentucky had Nunn. Want to be a Southern politician? It still pays to take a lesson from the blow george. Maybe two or three or four.

Which leaves us with the questions: how much has the blow george factor influenced the presidential campaigns of last fall and winter and this spring, how much effect will it have on the season of political conventions this summer, and what on earth might it do to us this fall? Lord knows enough people are weighing in already, but even the commonest of Common Taters has eyes.

ELISHA'S BEARS

I've been thinking more about my preacher friend who, as I mentioned a couple of weeks back, once took his congregation a bit too literally —or maybe too liberally—when the members told him to get real wine for a Communion service. He's now an educator, doing well in another state, and occasionally we still swap stories and laugh about our days as ministerial cubs back in the 1980s. The first time I ever went to preach to his flock for him, though, I don't recall laughing. Don't try guessing the name or location of the church; I'll never tell. Sweet Tater knows, and that's enough. And she won't tell either.

I arrived during Sunday School and seated myself at the back of the adult class to listen. The elderly teacher was lecturing on I Timothy 2:9-10, which speaks of the styling of hair and the wearing of ornaments. Want a further exposition? Look it up yourself. Right now I need only say that the teacher, though speaking in the mildest of tones, took a very conservative approach to the verses, more so than I would have done even at the time and much more so than I would now. But even though I thought he was a bit hidebound I knew that my own grandparents had shared his opinion exactly. If I could respect them, I could also respect him.

Not so, apparently, for at least half the class. I don't recall ever hearing an older individual addressed more rudely, harshly, or disrespectfully by such a large group of younger ones. Those who disagreed with the teacher acted as if he'd accused them of murder or something just as bad, and the walls echoed again and again with tearful cries of "Judge not, that ye be not judged!" and that tired, overworked old saw "The Lord knows my heart!" But through it all, the teacher responded with perfect old-time manners, returning smiles for glares and soft words for harsh. In so doing he earned not only my respect but my admiration. But he was a gentleman, and I—well, I'm just a common tater.

Finally one man dispelled the tension just a bit by telling a story about his wife's losing her wedding ring and her beheading of every chicken he owned to search their gizzards for it. That pretty much concluded the Sunday School, after which we had what passed for a worship service and the irked, flustered congregation sat through a fairly lame sermon by an extremely spooked young preacher. My pastor friend, however, appeared to be well accustomed to such shenanigans from his flock—likely they were most all family, which is about how such things work around here—but after the service ended and the crowd dispersed I observed to him that if the kids of Bethel had acted any worse to the Prophet Elisha than that Sunday School class had treated its teacher, I'd have hated to hear the racket. (II Kings 2:23-24. You can look that'n up too, preferably before reading on.)

"You know," my friend mused in reply, "I have trouble understanding that. The Bible says that Elisha cursed those little kids for mocking his baldness, and then two she-bears tore up forty-two of 'em for it! Would a God whose son said 'Suffer the little children to come unto me, and forbid them not, for of such is the kingdom of Heaven' really use a prophet so touchy about being bald that he'd cuss a bunch of little boys and girls for teasing him about it, and then have the Lord kill 'em with bears?"

I couldn't answer him right away, because at the time that one had me stumped too. Now I've come to view it as probably a memory some ancient scribe had of a cautionary tale his parents had told him as a child so he'd behave. When I was growing up my father had his own similar yarn, of a blue-nosed monster that lived in the well house and ate razor blades and broken light bulbs but preferred little kids when he could get them. Was Dad right for telling me and my cousins that story? Rest his soul, I don't hold it against him, and it for danged sure *did* keep us kids away from the well pump when we were little—which, of course, was exactly what Dad intended. I can smile even now thinking about him.

Sad to say, though, I heard the text of Elisha's bears all too often in sermons for years after this incident, first by yet *another* young preacher still in high school who'd been rebuked by an older one for skipping class, and in every single case afterward by similar speakers who were obviously peeved at somebody and just itching to sic the Prophet's bears on the perceived offender. If only people would just let them durned old bears hibernate! But if I recall right, on that long-ago day my final reply to my friend was something like this: "Well, you better be glad your Sunday School teacher didn't remember that Scripture and call out Elisha's bears himself—or then again, maybe the bears were already sitting in his class!"

THE REIGN OF KING MOB

Once upon a time in this great land of ours, the Common People felt that the Government ignored their voices. Hailing mainly from the states of the West of that day, such as Kentucky, Tennessee, Alabama, Illinois, and brand-new Missouri, these Common Men sent Congressmen to Washington, but their State Legislatures chose their Senators for them and most had grown up in a United States that, so far, had elected Presidents only from Virginia and Massachusetts. Wealth, position, and the East Coast seemed to hold unfair sway, and a just and truly representative Government seemed very remote.

But then a Savior came into view! In 1824 Andrew Jackson, horse racer, cock fighter, Indian killer, commander at the Battle of New Orleans, and now Tennessee Senator, was nominated by his State Legislature for President in the manner things were done back then. But politics quashed his initial hopes. He didn't get enough electoral votes to win the Presidency, and when the election was thrown into the House of Representatives his rival, Kentucky's Henry Clay, struck a deal with another rival, John Quincy Adams, to give his electoral votes to Adams in exchange for a cabinet post. For some reason the Kentuckian just didn't trust Jackson, and after Adams thus won the Presidency the Common Man's prospects for a voice in Government looked even bleaker than before.

Yet soon the Common Man could take heart! Jackson and his followers created their own brand-new political party, which then nominated Jackson again in 1828 and proceeded to storm the country! Though he was an immensely rich planter and slave owner, Jackson pointedly identified himself with the frontier soldiers who had served under his military command, and in fact Samuel Woodworth's "The Hunters of Kentucky," extolling the American Army's bravery at New Orleans, became his campaign theme song. And so in spite of a scandal uncovered by the snobbish, elitist Press that he had married his wife Rachel before she had secured a divorce from her first husband, with ballyhoo and hyperbole Andrew Jackson led his new political party, and his Common Men, to victory in the fall of 1828.

And the Nation was saved! So happy were the Common Men that thousands of them descended on Washington for the inauguration, and a grateful new President invited the entire street crowd into the White House for a reception. The Common Men, now assured that they had a voice in Government, trashed the Executive Mansion completely. The house staff managed to salvage what little furniture, china, and drapery they could by luring the crowd outside with tubs of spiked punch. Jackson's critics gloomily forecast that the White House punch party was only the beginning of the Reign of King Mob.

Okay, now let's omit the exclamation points. Jackson was no classical scholar, but he had extensive legal and military experience and he learned quickly from his Inauguration Day fiasco. Instead of being ruled by King Mob, for the most part he ruled King Mob and made King Mob like it. While he urged public participation in government, promoting suffrage for all white males at least, his administration actually increased Presidential power over Congress, and one biographer notes that he strained the concept of Democracy about as far as it would go and still remain workable. Historians still argue whether his financial policies led to the Panic of 1837 and the five-year depression that followed it, but Americans now mostly remember the Jackson Era fondly—excepting of course the Indian Removal Act of 1830. As one of my old high school teachers said, Jackson hated Indians with a purple passion, and a brief gold rush in Georgia gave him an excuse to compel Congress eventually to drive most of the Choctaw, Chickasaw, Cherokee, and other tribes across the Mississippi—making the United States the White Man's Country and resulting in more Indian deaths, and certainly more deaths of women and children, than the General had ever effected on the battlefield. One supposes that if a river was wide enough a wall wasn't needed. And Jackson could shove the blame for the entire process off his own shoulders onto the so-called Manifest Destiny of—you guessed it—the Common Man. Or King Mob; take your pick with names.

Do I do justice here to Andrew Jackson? In a brief column such as this I simply cannot, either for good points or bad, and he had a lot of both. Either way, he was a man of his times and not ours. And one of the biggest ironies in American history is that Jackson's political party eventually exchanged ideologies largely with the main descendant branch of the party that Henry Clay founded originally to oppose it. But I would voice one question for our own day: if King Mob ever elects another President, will that President then rule King Mob, or be ruled BY King Mob? Or will the Party of both President and Mob rule both President AND Mob? Whenever it may be, I suspect that King Mob's next reign will be just as cruel, unfair, shortsighted, and dangerous as any other time in our history that His Majesty has ever governed.

STANDUP GUY

In the summer of 1948 the citizens of the Big Sandy Valley were treated to an unusual diversion from the Dewey-Truman Presidential campaign: an undertaker fight. Now as a rule, undertakers aren't warlike. Even if the most persuasive preacher can't straighten you out while you're alive, undertakers will surely straighten you out afterward, and they're the very last folks who'll ever let you down. Still, the fracas occurred. A local mortician named Guy Preston ran a series of newspaper advertisements almost anticipating Jessica Mitford's controversial 1963 book "The American Way of Death," claiming that his industry largely overcharged its clients and offering what he termed as fairer prices for funeral services. As with Mitford's work later, the Kentucky Funeral Directors' Association at Louisville took a dim view of these ads, so its officers ran their own paid announcements locally in retaliation: they claimed that Preston's accusations were oversimplified and inaccurate, and ethical Kentucky undertakers who charged fairly were the rule rather than the exception. Even so, Guy had had his say, and although nowadays we might wince at his declaration that higher-priced funeral homes were run by "buzzards," his bluntness was surely a welcome contrast to the political hay being pitched elsewhere in the country that year.

But then again, Guy Preston was long accustomed to speaking his mind whether anyone else liked it or not—and often, they didn't. At least preachers. Years before, he himself had been an ordained minister and pastor in a local religious denomination, but he had been forced from the clergy and the church by circumstances largely beyond his control. Out from under the thumb of a restrictive religious hierarchy, though, he discovered a new voice. He founded his own newspaper of opinion that he called "Baptist Tidings," in which he became a spokesman for religious open-mindedness long before that quality became fashionable among his former clergy brethren. His editorial pen also gave him the opportunity to skewer many of these erstwhile brethren verbally for any acts of cruelty, hypocrisy, or just plain foolishness that he observed. And since we live in a country where the separation of Church and State and freedom of the Press are both guaranteed in the Bill of Rights, there wasn't a thing the clergy could do about him—except, perhaps, cry persecution.

One typical, and memorable, incident occurred during the darkest days of World War II.

A group of mothers, who belonged to various churches and in some cases perhaps no church at all, began to meet regularly to pray for their sons fighting overseas. The leadership of one sect took offense at its mothers praying together with women of other faiths in this fashion, and so brought several "sisters" up on charges for "walking disorderly," "departing from the Faith," or some such accusation and threatened to expel them from the church if they didn't stop their group praying. Sadly, we can't say at this point whether the accusers got away with this self-righteous little act of cruelty or not. A religious hierarchy, even merely a religious community, is still an intimidating force to many people in the Southeast, and no doubt was even more so, and to more people, back then. Though Preston now had the freedom he needed to speak his mind, the poor mothers still may have been either browbeaten into submission or kicked out of the church. Perhaps there were some instances of both. But regardless, Guy defended those women with every bit of strength he could put into his pen and paper, and he did not allow their persecutors to do one bit of their dirty work under cover.

Guy Preston died in 1952 and his newspaper, his ads, and the turmoil of a world war are all long past. Faded collections of "Baptist Tidings" still exist in the trunks and attics of a few local homes, and when I'm shown such treasure troves of community history I always encourage their donation to a public library for posterity's sake. I'm not sure I've ever convinced anybody to donate them, though. Some of the present owners of these collections may still be afraid of offending somebody either in their family or their church. "Baptist Tidings" was eagerly read by a lot of people in its day, but one still hears the occasional disparaging joke or story about Guy Preston, claiming that he had "the big head" and that he thought he was better than everyone else around him. But that's pretty much standard fare for anybody who stands outside the majority or the mainstream in a small rural community, and anyone with backbone enough to take an independent stance on any issue had better be ready for such accusations to come and go. Many of the predictions Guy made in his newspaper have come to pass, not because he had any prophetic gift—he'd have scorned that idea himself—but because he wrote with plain old common sense and a firm idea of the consequences of right and wrong. And in a day and age when so many politicians are trying to combine Church and State all over again for the sake of votes, oh Lord! We need voices like Guy Preston's more than ever.

A POCKETFUL OF FATHER'S DAY

As we near Father's Day, I've been thinking more of my dad. If he had lived until last month he would have been one hundred, and loving wordplay as he did it would have tickled him that his son had started a newspaper column called "The Common Tater." And since I have enough of my memories, and of his stories, on tap to make for many columns—and how I wish now I had asked him for even more of his recollections—I may as well start out with a brief tale, namely, the time he laughed the hardest and longest that I ever saw. Trouble was, I was the reason for it.

Dad's temper flared quickly but departed just as fast, or even faster. He held no grudges and in my childhood, if I could stay out of his reach for even half a minute, his temper would cool his intent down from a smack to a mere scolding. But a scolding from him was something special. He'd been a drill instructor at the beginning of World War II, and without even raising his voice he could combine just the right words to make either a mischievous kid or a smart-aleck teenager feel about two inches tall. And if he thought something I'd done was ridiculous enough to laugh at—oh Lord. There's no describing the humiliation. The prospect of that laughter kept me out of a lot of mischief.

Anyway, nobody on the two little creeks in our community had much land, but several folks tended gardens, a few had hogs, bee stands, and what not—and the main livestock, for those interested in keeping it, was the chicken, game or domestic. My grandfather and I raised both ducks and chickens for a while. So it happened one early spring—I was about nine—that circumstances made me the foster mother of a clutch of orphaned bitties that risked freezing if I kept them in the outside pen. Grandpa let me put a big old cardboard box in the back hallway next to his room, and after outfitting it with newspaper and jar lids filled with water and starter feed, I was ready to move my orphans indoors. And so, despite the fact that I knew I was doing what Dad called "picking up a lazy man's load," that is, carrying too much in one trip, I decided to bring all the bitties in at once, using my front pockets as well as my hands for the transit. I didn't lose a single bitty that way either, not even in the pockets although once I emptied them, I discovered a dividend in one that I should have expected—but hadn't. Dad came to look at the bitties just about the time I pulled out a sizable handful of the "dividend" and muttered disgustedly: "Well, them things (expletive deleted) in my pocket!"

Mom didn't hear me, and I was glad. Neither did Grandpa, for which I was gladder. But

Dad—I don't know how he threw back his head while simultaneously bending double and slapping his knees without rolling around on the floor, but he did it, and the laughter that emanated up and out from his belly absolutely laid it over anything I ever heard him do either before or after. As I mentioned, ridicule was the most effective discipline he ever used on me, but that time his laughter was so utterly infectious that I just had to join in or die trying not to. Now, when Mom saw the britches she'd have to wash, SHE didn't laugh, but although Dad got lots of mileage out of that story he always deleted the expletive that I let slip. It remained the one Mom didn't know about.

    I never quite knew what made Dad tick while he was alive, but at his funeral home viewing over Memorial Day weekend 2005—he'd lived twenty-six days past his eighty-ninth birthday, and had fussed continually since that birthday about "living too long"—many of his old co-workers remarked on his saying to them that back during the worst days of World War II he'd promised himself that if he ever got out of the

South Pacific alive he'd never worry about small things again. That cleared up many a mystery about him, but he took the talent for it with him to the grave and I sure wish I could have inherited it. Still missing you, Old Man.

THE SACRIFICE OF LUCINDA MILLS

Just recently I got word back from my preacher/teacher friend I mentioned in my previous columns about bootlegging and Elisha's bears: "You are quite the wit, or…at least half one." I can own up to that. It's pretty much the kind of banter he and I expect from one another, and his conversation almost always leaves me smiling. But the smiles are wry ones, because virtually all of our stories involve humans who, although they might search with all their hearts for transcendence, always end up acting very, sometimes poignantly, human. And some of the tales I've managed to collect over the years are not the stuff of comedy at all, but dire tragedy. I recall one of these today, shared with me not by my preacher friend, but rather by my father, who was sixteen when the events occurred and who remembered them all too well.

In early 1933, with so many Americans either starving or mad with worry at its prospect, an itinerant, independent evangelist, remembered by some as Anna Skaggs and others as Mary Scalf, began preaching on Rockhouse Creek in western Martin County. She collected a cult and even ordained a prophet. This prophet, John Mills, was said to be able to change water into wine and grapevines into snakes, and although few besides his immediate family joined the cult they stirred enough ruckus eventually to attract the national media. John's brother Leonard had been committed to Eastern State Hospital in Lexington, and to free Leonard from the State's care John determined that a human sacrifice was necessary, with the notion that God would restore the dead back to life within three days. It seems that at first Mills resolved to offer up four of his nieces, but the girls had enough sense to run away and either they or other neighbors notified the authorities. Some family accounts hold that the cult then considered sacrificing at least one infant, but after law officers arrived and removed the children—considering the worshipers' plans, the respect the peace officers showed for Freedom of Religion is amazing, if not extreme—Lucinda Mills, mother of John, Leonard, and other cult members, offered herself up for the sacrifice saying that she was willing to give her own life to get Leonard out of the asylum.

And so on February 8, 1933 John Mills laid his mother on a makeshift altar, caressed her with a Bible for awhile, then strangled her with a log chain as he spoke in supposedly unknown tongues. Too late to stop the sacrifice, the sheriff and deputies burst back in finally—some accounts claim the family was readying the body for burning—and arrested all the worshipers. On April 11, after a period in jail in which he alternated between violent rages and catatonic fits requiring a physician to break out two of his teeth with a chisel so he could be force-fed, John Mills was found guilty of homicide and was sentenced to life in prison. Two of the cult's other votaries were given sentences of 21 years apiece, and still more were acquitted, but all the guilty were eventually paroled. Mary Scalf or Anna Skaggs, or whatever the original instigator's name may have been, was never named in any of the indictments and got off scot-free. And now they're all dead, and that old common arbitrator Time has washed away most of the memory.

  Lucinda Mills was my grandmother Sparks' first cousin. I'd hoped to write a book about her sacrifice, but I was never able to figure out how without sounding sensationalistic. I've often wondered if Lucinda truly offered herself to get Leonard out of Eastern State, or simply to prevent John from killing her grandchildren. I'll never know. But we'd better be careful of thinking that nothing so perversely insane could ever happen again, or on a larger scale. Remember Jim Jones. The Hale-Bopp Cult. Ervil LeBaron and Warren Jeffs. The zealots that destroyed the World Trade Center who, whether or not Franklin Graham wants to admit it, worshiped the same God that good Jews, good Christians, and good Muslims all do. The rich televangelists who exhort you to send your last savings to them as "seed money" for the so-called Prosperity Gospel. Anytime humans don't use the single faculty that separates them from all other creatures, tragedy follows. The words an elderly cousin told me in 2001 still ring in my ears some nights, hauntingly: "We'd 'a' got her back if only the law hadn't busted in on us when they did."

JUST MY TEN CENTS' WORTH

Perhaps it's well that I try to stay a column or two ahead. Though I missed commenting on the tragic Orlando mass shooting immediately after it occurred, I can think before speaking. I wish some politicians would learn that running their mouths before they ascertain facts makes them sound stupid. But my own philosophy about gun control, and much else, largely takes the form of the George Santayana quote: those who forget the past are doomed to repeat it. And so in that spirit, and because it's still Father's Day month, I would recount a few interrelated stories from my old man, set back in the so-called good old days at the Royal Collieries mining camp at Offutt.

In the coal camps a holstered pistol was often simply part of a man's dress. Many men would even wear them to work, and boys would take them to basketball games up the creek at Meade Memorial. Dad could always make my downstate cousins laugh recounting this brief exchange he witnessed at the Offutt railroad station when he was ten or twelve years old: a self-proclaimed "bad man" stalked up to the ticket window, drew a big .45 hog-leg on the station agent, and barked, "Gimme a ticket to Paintsville!" Unfazed, the agent reached under the counter, pulled out his own .45, pointed it at his customer, and replied, "Ten cents, please." The guy paid up and walked off with his revolver and his ticket.

Truth is stranger than fiction. This really happened. But even Dad would admit that it sounded funnier in the glow of memory than it did when it actually occurred. Weekends in 1920s Offutt almost always involved bullets from every direction around that old train station, to the point that my grandparents absolutely forbade their boys to venture near it on Saturday nights. Even so, Dad witnessed homicides there as a child, and once peeked through a window to watch the mortician John A. ("One-Ear") Jones embalm one victim, a mine boss, so the body could be shipped back to Ohio on the train. For months afterward the favorite Offutt threat involved the promise of Mr. Jones' return to the train station to take similar care of the threatened person. Another mine supervisor and an innocent schoolteacher both caught in crossfire almost shared the same fate but for the quick actions of old Dr. F. M. Picklesimer, the company physician, who happened to be there. This was how my father grew up in the days of the free, unfettered observance of the Second Amendment, and even as late as 1951, long after Royal Collieries left Offutt, two of Dad's boyhood neighbors shot it out on the tracks right in front of my grandparents' home. He had to transport one of the bodies to the coroner in Paintsville in the back seat of his car. The place was truly no country for old men. Or all too often, for young ones, either.

Most of my knowledge about firearms came from Dad, that is, when he could get Mom off his back long enough to teach me anything at all. But then again maybe her fear of firearms was understandable: she grew up in Offutt too, and herself lost an older brother in a gun fight. I never became the expert shot that Dad was, but I learned to aim with both eyes open like he did, and how to care for pistols and rifles. He told me that the saddest words ever said were "I didn't know it was loaded," and although I never pressed him about it I suspect that maxim came from his childhood experiences as well. And he wouldn't carry a gun anywhere he didn't intend to shoot, because he always said that, except for a peace officer, anybody who went around packing heat all the time both looked and acted like a fool.

The Offutt in which Sweet Tater and I raised our kids was a lot less hectic, and at least somewhat more peaceful. But I think I can guess what my old man would say about Orlando, especially since, but for distance and circumstance, one of his granddaughters might have been among the casualties: good God. Will people ever show any common sense? How does the well-regulated militia of the Second Amendment equate to a completely unregulated mob? Do we really want to go back to the coal-camp days I knew growing up, when gun deaths were so common even little boys thought nothing of them?

Dad never forgot his past. But remember: those who do are doomed to repeat it.

HOSPITAL DRAMA

In thirty-four years of working in and around hospitals and clinics, I've collected a wealth of tales from what I've seen and heard, certainly enough to keep me writing for a long time yet—but I have to be careful how I present them. Short stories aren't much of a problem. All you have to do is fictionalize your names, settings, and dates to make sure nobody recognizes anything that actually occurred at a specific time and place. But nonfiction, even what's termed creative nonfiction, is another matter entirely, even here in eastern Kentucky where we live hip-deep in a conservative culture that actively requires gossip to maintain its customs and social mores. Not only is the betrayal of a person's confidential information illegal under the Health Insurance Portability and Accountability Act, it's simply not right, cuss and durn it. So over the years in recounting medical stories either comedic or tragic, I've developed similar guidelines. First, I use no real names, and if a given name becomes necessary I make note of the fact that it's a pseudonym—such as, say, Brother Drye in my bootlegger story. I suppose that for need I could call the other minister I've mentioned in that same column and a couple of others, the Rev. Elisha Beare; he agreed that I was at least a half wit, after all. Secondly, I let my stories marinate a few years before telling them, just enough to enlist the help of Father Time to make specifics a little fuzzier. Thirdly, I'm deliberately vague about location. In other words, what I want to do is convey the comedy or tragedy of the story's action itself, not make fun of anyone for simply being human. Between us all we have enough faults and failings to go around and fill up a dozen spare baskets besides, just like the good Lord with the loaves and fishes except we're multiplying mistakes rather than food.

So where to start, as a reference point? The best place I can see is the context that the great majority of my readers are probably most familiar with, not a real hospital itself, but the medical programs that are always available to watch on television or binge-watch on DVD. That may sound like a lost cause. After all, as law officers will tell you about 99.9% of police procedural shows, most of these are wildly inaccurate, and the "reality TV" emergency room programs are as bad as or worse than the dramas and soap operas. Sweet Tater can hardly stand to watch such a show with me because I usually criticize it indignantly from start to finish. And when the Tater Tots were at home they loved "Gray's Anatomy" every bit as much as I despised it. That made for some interesting conversations too.

But there are partial exceptions. Several years ago in a survey of law officers asking for an opinion of which police TV show depicted their own experiences most closely, of all the choices that were available the old 1970s sitcom "Barney Miller" won hands down. And in that spirit, I can honestly say that same thing about the hospital comedy "Scrubs"—not the zany plot twists or contrived lunacy in every script, though that's part of the show's appeal to me, but simply the general atmosphere of absurdity you know you're going to be dealing with every time you watch it. That's pretty much the same ambiance you can expect in a hospital on any given day, and the key to success is managing to pull something at least resembling sense out of the senseless. Maybe you have to have been there to understand what I'm trying to say, but at least to these middle-aged eyes "Scrubs" has the common everyday temperament of a hospital down pat. A lot of techs and nurses agree with me, too.

And so the old Common Tater just might start to bring up the occasional medical drama from recollection's vaults, always, rest assured, carefully self-edited. From the long-ago Independence Day a guy got so drunk he thought a firecracker was a cigarette and put it in his mouth and lit it and came to the ER with a couple of his teeth blown out, to the more recent holiday escapade wherein another drunk got the trigger of a pistol stuck in his belt buckle somehow and shot off something much more precious to him than teeth, I've often found my profession and my places of employment frustrating—but never boring. And by the way, happy Fourth of July, one day late.

THE RENAISSANCE MEN

I looked through my books the other day and found an old pamphlet that once belonged to my grandfather: a transcription of a lecture Dr. Paul B. Hall delivered at Louisville in 1964 entitled "My Forty Years' Practice of Medicine in the Hills of Eastern Kentucky." Skimming over it once again made me marvel how much the healthcare industry has changed, not only here, but all over the country, even since Dr. Hall delivered the lecture, let alone when he began his practice as a junior medical student back in the terrible, death-filled days of the 1919 Spanish influenza epidemic. Nowadays we have millions of drugs, tons of tests, and X-ray procedures enough to diagnose conceivably almost anything. Back in the days of his youth, Dr. Hall noted in the lecture, the drugs physicians could count on could be numbered on the fingers with digits left over, none antibiotics because those hadn't yet been developed, and he and his colleagues had to make virtually all their diagnoses using only their eyes, hands, and ears besides maybe a stethoscope and blood pressure cuff. So if it's true that a "Renaissance Man" is one who can boast of being accomplished in many disciplines, like Leonardo da Vinci with painting, sculpture and engineering all, our old-time country doctors were true Renaissance Men—at least from the standpoint of the dozens of subspecialties of medicine.

Besides the several stories about riding horseback through creek beds to reach patients and then later having his wife break the ice off the stirrups frozen to his feet, Dr. Hall recounted tales of surgical experimentation and innovation prompted by on-the-spot emergency decisions that would turn a typical young modern physician into a quivering lump of paralyzed fear. He often acted boldly because he just as often had no other choice. Nor was he the only mountain doctor forced to show audacity on a regular basis: though it's been a long time since the days of the coal company doctors, one still hears stories of mine accidents patched up almost MASH-style by these men, often fresh out of medical school and a one-year rotating internship and on their first jobs. I've already shared one anecdote of Dr. F. M. Picklesimer's days as Royal Collieries' physician at Offutt. Later on his partner in Paintsville for a while, Dr. A. D. Slone, diagnosed the first case of Rocky Mountain spotted fever ever reported locally, working from a set of symptoms that had stumped doctors much older than him. And though all had to be competent with a scalpel, arguably the neatest surgeon locally was Dr. E.G. Skaggs: he had a reputation for making the smallest, most precise incisions possible in any operation he performed, and once actually removed the appendix of one of my particularly skinny cousins using local anesthetic. Dr. Skaggs simply slapped a band-aid on top of the few stitches he left, and my cousin hopped off the operating table and walked, with a little assistance, back to his room. And the heroic, often wryly comedic, tales of the tough old doctors go on.

      The Renaissance Men's one great collective failing with their patients is almost understandable, though we're still paying for it today. Psychiatric disorders carried a terrible social stigma and hardly anyone would even admit to the possibility that they might suffer from such maladies. Even then, almost the only thing yesteryear's physicians could prescribe for cases of "nerves" was, simply, narcotic "nerve tonic." Later on pills took the place of the tonic, and over the years overworked doctors increasingly threw them at patients as quick fixes; one thing led to another until we have our present prescription-drug addiction crisis. And for all that, the country doctors of yore left a good, strong legacy of healing, one to which our own lawsuit-ridden modern healthcare profession might aspire. To those of us who work inside the industry, though, indoctrinated daily as we are with a medical philosophy that increasingly and evermore makes its very basis the initials C.Y.O.A.F.—like the Good Book says, he that hath an ear, let him hear; the first three letters stand for "Cover Your Own," and again to quote the Bible, the last shall be "First"—perhaps we are prone to view the deeds of the Renaissance Men somewhat through rose-colored glasses. The doctors of yesteryear would have given their eyeteeth for a full night's sleep, let alone the medical conveniences we now take for granted. I just can't help suspecting, though, if the Renaissance Men might have used them more fearlessly—and probably could have slept better, too.

BEARING ARMS IN CHRISTIAN AMERICA, PART ONE

Not too long ago I read a "quote," supposedly uttered by George Washington, that "free people need sufficient arms and ammunition to maintain a status of independence from their own government." Out of habit I looked up this "quote" in my favorite online fact-checking resource, Snopes.com, and was unsurprised to find it was just malarkey cooked up by open-carry zealots, made all the more odious by our most recent local gun tragedy. What was that my old man told me about the saddest words ever said… but if I'd thought another moment, I wouldn't have needed to check Snopes. I knew already that Washington, as President, had not only sent Federal troops into western Pennsylvania in 1794 to enforce an unpopular government excise tax on whiskey, but he'd actually ridden at their head—a rare instance of a sitting Commander-in-Chief personally leading an army into the field. One

"Whiskey Rebellion" leader, David Bradford, fled down the Ohio to territory still belonging to the French; another, a certifiable religious nut named Herman Husbands, the so-called "Pennsylvania Madman" who believed Heaven would soon descend on the far side of the Allegheny Mountains and who therefore thought his actions were all part of God's plan for the End Times, was sentenced as a traitor but then pardoned, possibly in consideration of his mental status; and despite all the high-blown rhetoric about God and Liberty mouthed by these men and others, resistance to Washington's army wilted. Thus the President managed to accomplish two things: he demonstrated that the National government was both willing and able to suppress resistance to its laws, an historical precedent the Confederates should have heeded in 1861 (Washington's army's second-in-command was General Henry Lee, father of General Robert E.); and the avoidable collapse of western Pennsylvania's whiskey industry gave that famous Kentucky Baptist preacher Elijah Craig's brand-new creation,

Bourbon, the chance to gain a place in the hearts of drinkers nationwide.

So, would our first President actually have approved of anyone arming against the established Government of the United States? Like Granddad Sparks would say, that notion and five cents will buy you a nickel cigar. Yet in another of history's ironies, no so-called open-carry patriot would dare blame Washington for enforcing Federal law. The Whiskey Rebellion and its defeat had to have been the fault of that old meanie, the United States' first Treasury Secretary, Alexander Hamilton, instead. Life is funny, that is, except when it's sad.

Still, this historical exercise led me to ponder individual freedom, Federal authority, and the history of arms control in the United States just a little further. I doubt that our ancestors would even be able to believe, much less understand, our current Second Amendment fights any more than they'd be able to comprehend that they were actually in a church house if they witnessed a modern worship service in a modern building, and I suspect that we would be just as confused if we could peer into the future at our own descendants. But gun control does in fact have a long history in the United States, and not just with the Western territorial marshals who forced travelers to the tough cow towns they guarded to surrender all firearms to their offices and deputies while within city limits. Clint Eastwood demonized this practice in the movie "Unforgiven," but in fact Wyatt and Virgil Earp and a host of other Western lawmen were guilty of it on a regular basis, and it probably prevented a lot more gun deaths than it ever violated anyone's rights. Let Eastwood talk about that awhile to an empty chair. But in fact, the first recorded American instance of firearms confiscation occurred before there ever was a United States, and it wasn't enforced by either the British Crown, the government of any American colony, or in fact any regularly constituted government at all. It happened in the fall of 1770 in that seedbed of Appalachian and Kentucky civilization, the backwoods of upland western North Carolina, and it was overseen by none other than that very same religious maniac who wreaked havoc in the Pennsylvania mountains a quarter century later with the Whiskey Rebellion, Herman Husbands. Even the Bourbon creator, Elijah Craig, was involved slightly too, though indirectly. Did I mention that life is funny? That is, except when it's sad?

More on this next week. But in addition to my favorite Santayana quote, you might consider another, this one verifiable from a later President, Harry Truman: the only thing new to you in the world is the history you don't know.

BEARING ARMS IN CHRISTIAN AMERICA, PART TWO

If ever a family man needed a dependable firearm, it was in backwoods, upcountry mid-1700s North Carolina. The colony's Royal Governor had just opened the area to settlement for an influx of Scots and Scots-Irish immigrants, and besides forests full of bear and panther, the Cherokee were only a few miles further west and colonial relations with them were volatile. But dangerous though things were, wild beasts and warriors weren't the backwoods families' only worries. They earned very little hard money, raising most of what they lived on and acquiring much of the rest by barter with neighbors, but they still had to pay taxes in coin to their county sheriffs —and it's doubtful one could find a crookeder set of "good ol' boys" anywhere. Even Governor William Tryon admitted that his upcountry sheriffs were among the worst embezzlers he had ever seen, and if they could successfully cheat the Governor himself we can only imagine their treatment of small farmers when they wanted to seize land for themselves. Upcountry North Carolina small landowners were truly between a rock and a hard place.

On, then, to the first American instance of gun control. About 1768 several upcountry farmers organized a "Regulation" to oppose the land-stealing of the sheriffs. At first these "Regulators" didn't rebel against Governor Tryon, much less King George; they only demanded fair treatment and equable taxation from their county officials, and referred to themselves as "Tories." But then the agitator Herman Husbands got involved with the movement. You'll remember Husbands and the 1794 Whiskey Rebellion from last week's column: he had himself convinced that the Second Coming would occur in colonial America, complete with the Holy City descending, and in order to realize this dream he was entirely willing to incite his listeners to his own hysteria—and their own violence. After Husbands joined the Regulation, his Doomsday predictions increasingly turned the group anarchic and savage.

    Luckily, Husbands wasn't the only upcountry religious voice. Baptists there were in plenty, and their leader, old Elder Shubal Stearns, whose musical pulpit style is still copied throughout Southern Appalachia today, was a pacifist strictly opposed to any anti-government violence. Among his younger preachers was Elijah Craig, also mentioned last week, and Elnathan Davis, whom Stearns likewise closely shepherded in the ministry, was moderator of a large church on Haw River. In 1769 Davis' congregation passed a resolution that any member taking up arms against the standing government should be excluded from fellowship. Regulation response was swift: Regulators promptly invaded the homes of every Haw River Church member, including Davis, and confiscated their rifles and muskets. One assumes they rationalized disarming their opponents, but the fact remains that the Regulators enacted the very first, and for years the only, recorded instance of gun control in American history. Ironically, once the American Revolution began, Regulator tales mixed with those of the Revolution and nowadays these gun thieves are often lionized as pre-Revolutionary patriots.

      The Regulator anarchy couldn't last. After Husbands' listeners destroyed the town of Hillsboro and burned Superior Court Justice Richard Henderson's barn and stables (the same man for whom Daniel Boone was then exploring Kentucky), Governor Tryon led an army west and defeated them at the Battle of Alamance Creek in May 1771. Afterward there was heartbreak to spare. Five Regulator leaders were hanged, the majority of Shubal Stearns' Baptists simply gave up trying to live in North Carolina and went further west to Tennessee, southwestern Virginia, and ultimately Kentucky, and that fall Stearns himself died—possibly of grief. Herman Husbands ran like a turkey to Pennsylvania just before the Battle of Alamance, saving his own skin while his hearers fell on the battlefield and died on the gallows. One wonders how much Husbands' fate in the 1794 Whiskey Rebellion involved karma, but old Preacher Stearns probably would have quoted Galatians 6:7 : "Whatsoever a man soweth, that shall he also reap."

Even more sadly, the questions raised by the Regulators' actions are still disputed. Would any God-and-Liberty-mouthing paramilitary "patriot" group in America today act differently than the Regulators if they managed to seize power —up to and including confiscating firearms from citizens who opposed them? And after all this time, haven't we had our fill of Doomsday predictions by lunatics claiming a direct line between God's voice and their ears? Apparently, not enough people think so. And I fear that before it's all over we'll relearn a hard lesson our Carolina ancestors took to heart more than two centuries ago.

Next week, I'll try to wind up this issue with something closer home and, hopefully, a little more cheerful.

APOCALYPSE NOW!

WE INTERRUPT THIS COLUMN FOR AN IMPORTANT ANNOUNCEMENT: THE APOCALYPSE IS COMING, and none of the Presidential candidates—not even *THAT* one—is the Antichrist. Nonetheless, it's on its way, and this man, the Common Tater, knoweth both the day and the hour: Saturday, August 6, from 10am to 6pm in Cynthiana, Kentucky, 22 miles northeast of Lexington on KY 353. *HEARKEN UNTO THE SOUND OF MY VOICE, YE READERS.*

I had wanted to wind up my gun control essays with the story of my old grandma and the time she lost a fight with her front door and a .32 Smith & Wesson double-action revolver, but I guess that'll keep till next week. After all, it's kept for forty-odd years already. For the present I have a story to tell about my work abode of nearly every weekend, Cynthiana, home of 3M's Post-It Plant; the Kentucky's Best Cigarette Factory; the E. D. Bullard company that makes industrial strength hard hats; a great many tobacco and horse farms; Harrison Memorial Hospital (finest rural healthcare gig I ever worked, too: quality patient care, a Board of Directors and Management attuned to the needs of working professionals, and best of all, no blatant eastern Kentucky-style nepotism); and, as I found out only recently, the genuine birthplace of the pop cultural phenomenon known as *The Walking Dead.*

That's right. *The Walking Dead.* And the whole thing got its start in, of all places, the Bluegrass State. Tony Moore, the original artist of *The Walking Dead* in its pre-American Movie Classics Network days as a comic book series, happens to be a native of Cynthiana, and he set the beginning of the great and notable Day of the Zombie Apocalypse in Room 251 of the very hospital that graces his dear old home town—and where I work. Even Moore's sketches of the outside of the hospital building and the grounds in the comic's first issue are true to real life. And so this coming Saturday the city of Cynthiana, in conjunction with Harrison Memorial, will host its very own Walking Dead Festival with the theme of "Where It All Began." I've already heard that every hotel and motel in Lexington, Georgetown, Paris, and Cynthiana itself is booked solid by eager fans of both the comic and the television series. It's possible that we could see a crowd of as high as ten thousand this weekend, though it's a daunting prospect to think of the majority of them dolled up like rotting corpses for their tour of the fateful Room 251 at the hospital and through the rest of the city. I have to admit to my own particular dread at the possibility of hundreds of cases of heat exhaustion, along with the aftereffects of however many impromptu fights between avid fans, flooding our Emergency Room, and the idea of seeing teeth marks on scalps is—well, let's just say if that occurs it'll really put us hospital workers in the genuine spirit of the thing. Especially if some joker gets too far into his roleplaying and decides he wants to try out the flavors of OUR brains. But I've already told you in a previous column: the essence of life in any hospital is its unceasing and consistent absurdity, so I'm ready to ride along with a big smile. For one Saturday, at least.

Should the city of Cynthiana be this eagerly supportive of an artist who has so deftly exploited his own hometown to begin the tale of a science fictional world disaster? Well, why not? After all, no publicity is bad publicity and if Samuel Johnson was correct, anyone who writes for any other reason than money is a fool. I myself cherish my tiny royalty payments and even the little dab that the good folk of Around Town pay me for Commontatering. By Johnson's definition, Tony Moore and his original partner in the Walking Dead venture, Madison County native Robert Kirkman, are thus as eligible for a place in Kentucky's literary pantheon as Jesse Stuart and Robert Penn Warren. Besides that, I prefer out-and-out over-the-top sci-fi to a great deal of the fiction-posing-as-fact scribblings I've seen lately from from so many Appalachian, including Kentucky, authors. A. J. Offutt always could write better than that son of his anyway. I think Moore and Kirkman have done great by themselves. So if you're into the story line of The Walking Dead, this weekend hit the Parkway, set the GPS, and enjoy. Fresh apples in Paintsville the first weekend of October, fresh brains in Cynthiana the first weekend of August. What could be better? Come on down!

GRANDMA AND THE SECOND AMENDMENT

My three previous gun-control columns have been more or less solemn and earnest, but I find that I simply can't leave the issue until I add something a little more lighthearted—although down deep, this story is as serious as the others. It involves the first time I ever personally witnessed a Second Amendment violation, but it also has the bonus of allowing me to recount a memory of one of the few times I ever had a laugh on my father rather than the other way around. Even so, I was a bit too intimidated at the time to laugh myself. You'll see why.

Dad's mother was, well, memorable—perhaps not so much so as her first cousin Lucinda about whom I've already written, but unforgettable nonetheless. I don't remember a time growing up when Grandma wasn't dying of some horrible disease or other, and sadly, one of her ailments finally caught up with her two months before her ninety-fifth birthday. Smile if you will at that. I was twenty then, and in spite of all the times she'd threatened to die, I still mourned when she actually went ahead and did it. I wonder how long she'd have lived if she hadn't smoked like a freight train all those years.

After my grandfather Sparks passed away, Grandma moved from Offutt to another community nearer Paintsville. Her new home was bordered closely by a church and three other houses, one of these belonging to the congregation's minister (a cousin) and another to one of her nieces. In spite of this snug, comforting presence of God and kin, though, she still slept with Grandpa's old Smith & Wesson 32-caliber "yaller jacket" under her pillow, and it was unwise to step onto her porch after dark without calling first. One night she thought she heard a prowler, got up, drew the revolver, and emptied it into her front door. Trouble was, she'd tried to sight down the barrel of the .32 as if it were a rifle—at least that's how Dad figured it afterward—and consequently temporarily lost the hearing in her right ear. I learned how to shoot using that old gun myself, and a small cannon couldn't have had much more of either volume or recoil.

After a relative telephoned us Dad rushed to the scene, worried about bullet holes not only in cousins' houses but in cousins too. He had me come with him; if it wasn't for moral support I'm not sure why. Thankfully, we found no casualties except the door and Grandma's ear, and nobody'd even called the law—gotta love family—but Dad was mightily irked about Grandma's carelessness with the gun and he began to try to lecture her on firearm safety. That's when the real trouble started. Grandma was hardly ever at a loss for a reply to anything or anyone, but she absolutely could not hear out of her right ear for days afterward and about every ten words out of Dad's mouth she'd interrupt him with a loud "HUH?" He'd increase his volume for another sentence or so, then get another "HUH?" in reply, and so after the sixth or seventh "HUH?" he was speaking as loudly as I ever heard him talk in my life, his jawline was an alarming shade of dark crimson, and his blue eyes were flashing fire. I just tried to listen and not say a word—for the most part, Dad was one of the most even-tempered men I ever knew, but when his patience was tried too far you wanted to climb a tree before asking what was wrong—and stifle my laughter at the situation he and poor old Grandma were caught in. I think some of the cousins got tickled too, and like me, were trying their best not to show it. Nobody dared look at each other. The whole thing really wasn't funny, yet it was hilarious. I think the Germans call this kind of thing "schadenfreude," but Teutonic title or no, it was pure eastern Kentucky.

At the end of Dad's rebuke Grandma said "HUH?" again. At that point Dad just gave up and confiscated the pistol, I helped Grandma pack her things together, and we locked her well-ventilated door and brought her home with us. Technically, Dad thus violated Grandma's Second Amendment rights, but looking back, I don't think the strongest gun enthusiast in the world would have dared say a word about it to his face at the time. Like the proverbial skeleton afraid to cross the road, nobody in their right mind would've had the guts.

QUOTATION REMARKS

My biggest regret as a Common Tater is that, no matter how hard I try to persuade Sweet Tater, she won't let me quote her in my column. She feels that our conversations are confidential and should remain that way. Although I've even offered to attribute all her sayings to "my first wife," for some reason she doesn't like that idea either. But I guess I really can't blame her. She's right; I do need to keep our private communications private. But then technically, I guess I've actually just now quoted her. You can't win sometimes.

Even so, and though she be unquoted, Sweet Tater remains my constant inspiration. I don't mean to say that like some sanctimonious blow george in the pulpit on Sunday morning, either. Every time I hear a preacher start showering his wife with sugary, lovey-dovey compliments during a sermon I want to ask him—and her, too—if her familiarity with his private conduct ever prompted her to shout and rejoice and shake hands with the sisters while he was up sermonizing. In twenty-odd years of churchgoing and pastoring I never saw such a phenomenon from Sweet Tater, nor did I expect to. She knew, and knows, me too well for such as that. But I guess the main reason she's inspirational to me is the fact that, though we lock horns and butt heads from time to time like people with strong opinions must, more often than not she and I find ourselves in a conspiracy against the rest of the world—and once in a while, that very conspiracy itself takes a wry, humorous turn on its own. She's a wonderful co-conspirator, whether we're conspiring or being conspired against, or both.

To illustrate, I'll tell the story of a sermon that she and I once heard together. For the record, it wasn't from either Brother Drye or Brother Beare, but rather an out-of-state guest one Palm Sunday years ago at a church I pastored. He began his discourse by telling the Palm Sunday story from the twenty-first chapter of Matthew in the King James Version of the Bible, a portion of which reads (verse 5): "Behold, thy King cometh unto thee meek, and sitting upon... a colt the foal of an ass." Meaning, of course, in the Shakespearean English of the good old King James, that Jesus rode into Jerusalem on a young donkey, but that morning my visitor tried to quote that particular verse from memory—and he got the words "foal" and "ass" exactly backwards. I was sitting behind him in the pulpit and so he couldn't see my facial expression when I heard that Our

Lord had entered Jerusalem perched on the southern end of a northbound foal, but I looked over to the sisters' section of the congregation at Sweet Tater, she looked back at me, and both of us lifted songbooks almost simultaneously to hide our faces. We couldn't hold our hymnals there forever, though, and so I think we passed the rest of the service wearing broad grins which I suppose we both hoped appeared indicative to everybody else of how happy we were in our salvation that blessed morning. After the service was over I couldn't even bear to point out Brother Foale's misquote to him in private; he was always very serious and earnest in his conduct and thus it would have been too embarrassing for both him and me, and in any case I couldn't have repeated what he said with a straight face if my life had depended on it. Even now I can't. I still laugh out loud almost every time I think about the incident, this many years later. But that evening Sweet Tater and I became reflective, and sad as well, when we realized that of all the people in attendance at church that morning, we were the only adults even to notice that we'd been "blackguard-ed," as the old folks' saying went, by an ordained minister. Nobody else was paying close enough attention to the preacher's words to pick up on the gaffe. So maybe the biggest, dirtiest joke was on the pastor and his wife, after all.

Oh, well. At least Brother Foale didn't infuriate my flock by mentioning any Bible verses about makeup or divorce. That's something, anyway. I won't quote any of mine and Sweet Tater's discussions on those two subjects, but one day I may tell you how another minister burbled verbally over Ephesians 6:16's "fiery darts of the wicked"—if I can just figure out how to word it in a family newspaper.

BLACKGUARDIN'

The final portion of last week's column prompted me to reflect some more about my use of a truly characteristic eastern Kentucky verb: that being, to blackguard. Any good dictionary will tell you that a blackguard (the noun, in most areas of the English-speaking world pronounced "blaggard," with a silent "ck") is "a person, particularly a man, who behaves in a dishonorable or contemptible way" or, quite simply, a time-honored synonym for a scoundrel. But you can only find the verb form of the term, that is, to blackguard (in this usage pronounced just like it's spelled), in lexicons of archaic English, and it means "to abuse someone in a coarse, insulting manner, often humorously." In short, in the eastern Kentucky of only a few years ago, the old Anglo-Saxon terms for the derriere as noted in my last week's musings, the acts of defecation, flatulence, urination, and procreation, and the two short synonyms for female dogs that come to mind, for example, weren't cuss words, exactly: rather they were blackguardin', though they were certainly looked upon by most folks with little if any more favor than the strictly cussin' words one might utter in violation of the Third Commandment or the Sermon on the Mount's injunction to "swear not at all."

Even the Kentucky judicial system once made a distinction between cussin' and blackguardin'. At one time uttering a profane oath in court guaranteed, and perhaps still guarantees, a bench-imposed fine; though not entirely accurately, this misdemeanor was once referred to legally as blasphemy, and there's an old story still floating around local courthouses about some poor guy who was fined a dollar for blaspheming, had only a five-dollar bill in his pocket for which the bailiff couldn't make change, and so therefore decided to cuss out the judge for four more dollars' worth of profanity. But in one of the last documented proceedings involving "bad" language ever to be tried in a Kentucky court, featuring an outspoken Knox County female moonshiner who'd openly identified the County Attorney prosecuting her case as the offspring of a female dog, the Kentucky Court of Appeals found in the woman's favor in this particular because her choice epithet didn't strictly involve blasphemy as such: in the exact (but slightly censored) words of the March 7, 1952 ruling, "When a gentleman speaks to a lady possessing Mattie's rugged personality he should not be abashed if she calls him a son of a (expletive deleted). He should merely consider it one of the vicissitudes of life and go on his way rejoicing, comforted by the thought that women are often mistaken." Chauvinistic, I know, but it's probably the very thing that County Attorney needed to hear, especially if he was throwing the book at poor Mattie for engaging in one of the few ways she could eke out a livelihood on a thin-soiled hillside farm. At one time even in this county, not to mention Kentucky's other hundred and nineteen, one could do more jail time for chicken stealing than homicide, depending on one's family's political connections. Reckon that's still the case?

Anyway: language inevitably evolves over time. When the King James Version of the Bible was translated, the most commonly-known current blackguardin' word for urination was still considered acceptable for polite conversation and even public reading matter (for example, see I Samuel 25:22 and Isaiah 36:12). The King James remained the most widely-accepted English translation until the mid-twentieth century, and yet the repressive Comstock Anti-Pornography Postal Laws of the late 1800s and early 1900s made it technically illegal to send a Bible through the mail because it had that word in it—though, as we can easily imagine, the puritanical Postmaster General Anthony Comstock's censors ignored that one little indelicacy because it was the Bible, after all. But it's hard to say what the future holds. Television networks have openly broadcast common cuss words for years now, and every day the majority of them are "bleeping out" fewer and fewer terms that we usually define as blackguardin'. Might the polite speech of our descendants one day sound as foreign, and as coarse, to us as that of our ancestors who spoke the English of the King James Bible? Will the so-called F-bomb and S-word finally come full circle from ancient Anglo-Saxon and be termed as "good English" once more? And by that time, and with those terms added back in, will the language even be worth speaking or writing, that is, if anybody's still even being taught to write on paper rather than using a keyboard?

(Expletive deleted) if I know. I'm just a Common Tater.

THE "A" WORD

Word day for the second week in a row in the Tater Patch, folks, and although the term under consideration today isn't particularly eastern Kentuckian, it goes back to the dawn of human culture itself: *ANTHROPOMORPHISM*. Call it the "A" word for short if you like, but thankfully, it's a lot more easily defined than spelled: basically, when you think or speak of a thing or an animal as if it were human, you've anthropomorphized it. The Book of Job says that "the morning stars sang together" at the Creation (38:7), and even before Aesop wrote his fables, talking and human-reasoning animals were already the stock of children's stories. If the "A" word isn't an inborn psychological tendency in humans it's certainly a time-honored practice in child-rearing: parents and educators try to teach kids basic life lessons from stories such as the Little Red Hen, the Ant and the Grasshopper, and the Three Little Pigs, and as the kids mature, hopefully they accept the fact that although the animal fables are just that, fables, the principles behind the tales are still sound and worth keeping.

I suspect, though, that the "A" word has finally reached its low point. At least I hope so. Over the centuries we've gone from oral tales to storybooks, books to animated cartoons, cartoons to computer-generated films, and just recently a brand-new creation of this type, "Sausage Party," has been released to movie theaters. It's a story about living, thinking groceries who conceive of humans as gods that buy them to care for them in the Great Beyond, but who find out the hard way that their real fate is to be cooked and eaten. Its violence and gore make the shootings and explosions of yesteryear's cartoons appear tame by comparison, not even to mention its graphic sex and language, and although it's billed as strictly R-rated adult fare, the kids of parents either too lazy or preoccupied to care for them properly will still watch it—if not in movie houses with these same lazy or preoccupied parents, then either on pay-per-view, cable, or DVD while the aforementioned lazy, preoccupied parents amuse themselves otherwise. At least my own Tater Tots are grown, so in any case I won't have to do any explaining that, our status as Taters notwithstanding, peeling a potato is not the equivalent of flaying a human being alive, noodles aren't really a soup can's entrails, and baby carrots don't actually shriek in terrified little-girl voices for their mommies when you pop them into your mouth. How long do you actually think it'll be until we see "Sausage Party" collectible figurines and stuffed toys on the market, R-rating notwithstanding? I'm betting Christmas.

But "Sausage Party" isn't the only way we've misused the "A" word—and strange as it may sound, its script writers aren't even entirely wrong. In the story, the groceries think of humans as gods, and in reality, what do humans do? Mostly, we keep an A-word concept of our Maker that's very little clearer or better than the childhood view from which we congratulate ourselves that we've matured. Not only is this the real reason terrorists crash airplanes into buildings in the name of God, but also why there are so many fights and so much gossip and bad blood in individual churches while everyone still claims to "love one another." As humans, we imagine God as some super-HUMAN endowed with both our best and worst qualities, and then both preach His love and proclaim intolerance in His name because we're too terrified of our own concept of Him to dare omit the practice of either. Could this split personality to which we've A-worded the Creator actually be the worst kind of blasphemy? In the words of Asaph in Psalm 50:21, quoted here from the Revised Standard Version for clarity rather than the King James, God accuses the wicked that "you thought that I was one like yourself." So maybe it's time that we actually took this to heart along with I Corinthians 13:11, that "when I was a child I spoke as a child, I understood as a child, I thought as a child; but when I became a man, I put away childish things." Asaph the Psalmist and Paul the Apostle were more correct in these passages than even they knew—or than we do. We all need to grow up, accept that it's better to have questions we can never answer than answers we can never question—and start acting like the adults we claim we are. The "A" word, like cartoons, is for kids.

PULPIT POLITICS, PART ONE

As a paid Common Tater, when I write about current politics I try to be neutral. To paraphrase Merle Haggard, if you want to see the partisan side of me, check Facebook. But I'm still an equal-opportunity critic and an ex-preacher both, and at the risk of sounding like Earl Pitts, American, one thing that makes me sick at heart and stomach both is to see secular partisan politics of any sort get into a house of worship. Church politics is a repulsive enough mess on its own, comparable to sausage in a way: if you like it, make sure you never watch it being made. But when you add secular issues into the religious mix it becomes an evil greater than the sum of its parts, more like a cowpile: the harder you stir it, the worse it stinks. And with the active encouragement of evangelists both on and off television, eager to acquire political power for their own personal gain and skilled in the ways of the Ephesian silversmiths described in the nineteenth chapter of Acts—working a crowd until some cry one thing, some another, the majority doesn't even know what's really going on but everybody's as mad as wet hens about *SOMETHING*—nowadays it's happening more and more all the time.

    I've written about one basic example of this type of thing already: the last local-option vote and its accompanying hyperbolic prophecies of drunks passed out on every corner and strip joints lining Main Street if the city should "go wet," both sides of the issue getting mightily angry at one another but neither threat ever materializing. Occasionally, too, in this Internet age you hear of a church posting sermons online that are partisan politically, causing the IRS to warn the preacher that he's risking his church's tax-exempt status and ultimately making a hullabaloo community-wide because the government's supposedly persecuting the poor man of God and making him a martyr for his faith. I can think of a few choice four-letter responses to this idea, the cleanest of which is "bunk." There's no martyrdom, or even suffering, involved here. If any church and/or preacher wants to tell people whom to vote for all they need to do is voluntarily give up their tax exemptions and pony up like the rest of us. Then they can "electioneer" completely legally, but I don't see anybody giving up any tax exemptions any time soon, religion, bunk, or no.

Still, neither of the above examples qualify as the worst local church-and-state violations ever to occur. I've often heard my folks speak of the 1960 Presidential contest when at least one community congregation actually sent its members door-to-door to campaign against John F. Kennedy: as one of those dreaded (back then, anyway) Roman Catholics he'd surely let the Pope take over the country. Al Smith was accused of the same thing in 1928 when he ran against Herbert

Hoover. In Kennedy's case, though, voters didn't need to worry so much about the Pope as they did the Pop. If old Joe Kennedy hadn't had a stroke between Election Day 1960 and Inauguration Day 1961 I suspect that his sons—both President John and Attorney General Bobby—would have hopped every time their old man said "frog." Then again and for all we know, if old Joe had stayed healthy he might have kept John away from the Bay of Pigs and both sons might have lived longer and done more good. Who can say? In any case, in 1960 White Anglo-Saxon Protestant churches all over the country attempted similar anti-Kennedy/anti-Catholic campaigns, not only in eastern Kentucky, and none ultimately affected the election. And nowadays, only the most extreme hen-house sects have anything ill to say about Roman Catholic candidates, or even those of other non-Protestant faiths—except Islam, of course, which is still freely criticized around here in spite of all the Muslim physicians and their families who've been good citizens in this area for decades. For the 2012 election the Billy Graham

Evangelistic Association actually removed all the anti-Mormon rhetoric from its website in honor of Mitt Romney's Presidential run. I suppose in some way you can call that progress. I never checked to see if Franklin and Anne put it all back on the site after Romney lost.

And then twenty-odd years ago there was that young fool of a pastor that—but I guess we'll just have to finish that story next week, won't we? Stay tuned. I'm like the little boy that ate too many green apples about this one: you see, I've got inside information.

PULPIT POLITICS, PART TWO

William Faulkner remarked in a novel that the past is never dead; it's not even past. For some reason that quote's stuck with me through several years, juxtaposed oddly in my mind with a statement from one of the old preachers who ordained me: once he observed to me that he had never, ever known how mean folks could really be until after he joined the church. I thought he was teasing me, in the rough manner older men used to rib young ones and maybe still do, but when I looked into his eyes I realized he was completely serious—and I couldn't think of a single reply. The past isn't even past, and how mean folks can be: all of it comes together for me in the tale of my single foray into mixing religion and politics as a pastor, and I still kick myself over the fool I was.

For years, the ratio of Republicans to Democrats in Johnson County was almost identical to the proportion of men who fought for the Union in the Civil War (Republicans, the majority) versus those who joined the Confederates (Democrats, the minority). And so, more than a century and a quarter after Appomattox, I found myself pastoring a church just across Levisa Fork from one of the few Democrat precincts in heavily Republican Johnson County: Greasy Creek, which also included Banjo Creek a little further downriver and which had once even been known as the Little Confederacy. It didn't matter much that the Democrats and Republicans had almost completely switched political philosophies over the years, either. Several of my older members who lived nearest the church were as hardcore Democrat as you could get, their opinions solidified all the more by the Great Depression. Now, if you remember the 1980s and 1990s you know that several prominent televangelists had by then largely succeeded in branding one political party good and the other evil in the South's public consciousness, but that didn't matter to these folks. They felt like they knew right from wrong, and nobody would change their minds. And in any case, you didn't talk about stuff like that in church. It was bad manners.

Just my luck, I had a visiting preacher that tried it. He was another out-of-stater like Brother Foale, though not from the same state, but evidently it was a place where that kind of pulpit talk was becoming accepted even within a traditionalist rural sect like ours. But when he started lambasting the President, my old members, especially the sisters in the left-hand corner right below the pulpit, suddenly went white around the mouth with indignation and started glaring daggers at him. They may not have paid any attention to Brother Foale's Palm Sunday text but they sure picked up on this other fellow's comments quickly enough, and I don't recall ever seeing a bunch of sweet old ladies giving a preacher more baleful looks during a worship service in my life. My mind raced. What to do, grab the man's coattail and seat him and shut him up? Sing him down, maybe? Both were historically valid options in our sect's practice and I'd even done the latter once, but either could still cause a scandal and so in the interests of what I thought at the time was peace I waited on him to finish as patiently as I could, followed his sermon up with one of my own, and soon made my old sisters happy once again by criticizing the wife of a former President, of the other political party of course, for consulting astrologers. One thing must have canceled out the other in my members' sensibilities, and most were once again willing to shake the visitor's hand when the service was over. And for whatever it was worth to either of us, the Presidential critic was willing to shake the pastor's hand too.

So who was the better man, him or me? Looking back, we both appear pretty sleazy in my estimation, and I'm still every bit as ashamed of and disgusted by the incident and my response as I was the day it happened. Hindsight's twenty-twenty but now I wish I'd simply grabbed that man's coattail and seated and silenced him, especially since he later did more to prove to me how right my older colleague was than any other man I ever worked with. Live and learn, I guess. This November if I see anybody in the blind man's ditch from a similar blunder you can bet I'll be offering a sympathetic hand up rather than a self-righteous foot down.

SQUIRREL & MUSLIMS—or, AyMAYun?

When I preached, I was never the type to holler out *"ayMAYun?"* during sermons as if I wanted or expected a congregation to shout it back to me in approval. (That's "amen" for you non-natives; it's just how preachers often pronounce it around here, don't ask me why. Some of 'em quote "the Boible" at "waship" services too.) Still, considering how often I've heard that trick used, such responses must be gratifying, although they depend largely on a congregation's mood. And yet for all the satisfaction *"ayMAYuns"* may provide, the question lingers: which is better, honesty or popularity? Should one always tell the truth of one's conscience, even if it provokes a houseful of scowls, or say something non-controversial and witty—or half-witty—for the quickie *"ayMAYun?"*

If you read The Common Tater, you already know how I settled that question for myself. But if I wrote a religious column and wanted to take the easy road to an easy-as-pie *"ayMAYun,"* all I'd need to do is condemn Muslims. Around here they're completely safe to criticize. No matter that we've had Muslim residents in this neck of the woods since the 1980s and before, most of them hard workers and good citizens: the 9/11 terrorists were Muslim, Saddam Hussein was Muslim, Osama bin Ladin was Muslim, and so Muslims as a group are perceived in today's American South to be as dangerous as the Russians were back when I was growing up. Any challenge to the common perception is met with hostility, if not accusations of heresy or worse. But after you've seen one Baptist deacon draw a pistol on another in a church parking lot over a disagreement that didn't merit even a moment's consideration from either, let alone threats, it gets a little tough to hurl stones at another religion; and since the pistol-pulling incident happened at approximately the same time I began working with Muslims in the healthcare industry, 1982, I thought I'd offer an anecdote about the single time in thirty-four years I ever heard a Muslim acquaintance set his religion apart in any opposition to the majority opinion of our area.

It happened at the second hospital I worked in, with a young Muslim physician "taking call" for an old GP who was going off to hunt squirrel. The two met in the ICU where I was drawing blood, and as I worked nearby the GP thanked his substitute for the favor, promising to bring him a mess of squirrel upon his return. The younger doctor looked embarrassed and, obviously choosing his words carefully, began to explain why Islam's dietary laws forbade his family's eating squirrel: their Imam (another doctor there) had to verify that the animals had died without pain, etc., to which the old GP replied with an understanding smile, "Oh, I get it! You're *KOSHER!*" That produced a laugh from the Muslim, who answered, "Yeah, something like that!"

And that's all there was to it. No acrimony whatsoever. And a great many of us on the first floor enjoyed the observance of Ramadan that year too, though we weren't Muslims. That young doctor's wife was a night-shift ER nurse, and during Ramadan she brought in enough good food for after-sundown dining to gorge us all.

But what about bin Ladin and ISIS, you may ask? Well, what about that sneakin' deacon with the pistol, and how much damage might he have done if some good Christians with common sense hadn't restrained him? But he wasn't a TRUE Christian, you may protest. TRUE Christians don't act like that. Really? The old fool had made a good enough testimony to get ordained as a deacon, hadn't he? He claimed that night that the sheriff had told him it was okay to pack the gun, and if true, that may have kept him out of jail. My point is, you can find good people and stupid, violent people in any religion; their actions, not their creed, make the only difference that counts. I can understand why anybody unfamiliar with Muslims might be afraid of them, and I'd respond, well, go see one or two of the local doctors then, and rest easy. What really disgusts me is to see people who've worked with Muslims as long as, or longer than, I have, mouth the same paranoid rhetoric you hear from people who don't know any better.

But who knows? Right now at least one major American political party seems to think that the Russians have become just the nicest guys ever, so maybe there's hope that some day anti-Muslim prejudices might fade too.

AyMAYun?

APPLE DAYS, ASSOCIATIONS, AND YELLOW JACKETS

The Kentucky Apple Festival is once again upon us, and while Johnson County welcomes most visitors we must also acknowledge those we aren't so eager to see: the white-faced hornets, or yellow jackets as they're known locally, whose population is always at its highest this season and whose numbers at the Apple Day festivities rival those of the humans. And whenever I think of yellow jackets or any other similar stinging insects, I always recall my father with a smile. I've said before that Dad was one of the calmest, most sensible men I ever knew, but if there was one thing that made him react from the gut rather than his head it was a wasps', hornets', or yellow jackets' nest anywhere near our place.

I'm not certain why. Dad wasn't a beekeeper, but he liked honeybees and didn't want them bothered. He liked bumblebees because he said they were the only insects that could pollinate red clover. He tolerated dirt daubers too, because they hardly ever sting, and I can recall him when I was young, showing me a dirt dauber dragging a katydid to its nest as food for its larvae. But as far as he was concerned it was open season on most other such pests with nests. Grandma (yep, the same Grandma who air-conditioned her front door with the Smith & Wesson) used to say that once when Dad was little, he'd put on a shirt with several "waspers" hidden inside it and he'd harbored a grudge against them and all their kind ever since. She may have been right. But I do know for sure that, while our neighbors mostly used common sense in destroying a wasps', hornets', or yellow jackets' nest, waiting until dark for all the insects to return and then squirting gasoline on it or in it, invariably killing them immediately, Dad would march right out to any nest he found during the sunniest part of a hot summer day armed only with a fly swatter. He'd knock down or break open the nest depending on its location, jump back, and start swinging that fly swatter like a knight wielding a sword against a fire-breathing dragon until both he and his winged,

stinged adversaries were worn tea-totally out. He
never wanted me along on these pesticide
missions, perhaps fearing that I was, unlike him,
allergic to insect venom, but I wasn't really all that
crazy about joining in the fight anyway. Many's
the time I've watched him from a safe spot and
when he'd finally turn back toward the house with
a big grin I knew he'd scored another victory.
Sweet Tater's seen him do it too, both before and
after she and I married. Mom always quarreled at
Dad as she applied vinegar to his stings,
wondering out loud and loudly why he always had
to turn pest control into a battle royal, but he'd just
smile at her as if to say: fuss to your heart's
content, darlin', you can't take my triumph away
from me.

      Though I'm no more allergic to stinging
insects than Dad was, I still prefer a more subtle
approach to dealing with them. I once described
my favorite method to another preacher, years ago
at a church association meeting. Like the Apple
Festival, association time is always in late summer
or early fall when the yellow jackets are busiest,

and on this occasion the host congregation had set up several tents and long picnic tables outdoors for the crowd's lunchtime accommodations. Trouble was, the yellow jackets were out in force and seeking fellowship too, and they pretty much insisted on taking communion with us that afternoon. It was no love feast, either: everybody was on guard for yellow jackets hiding in their sandwiches and floating in their pop. As I waved a couple of the buzzing pests away from my drink I observed to the brother clergyman nearest me, "You know, if the moderator of this church had thought about it two weeks ago he could have solved this problem."

"How?" he asked, batting at several more yellow jackets hovering over his dessert.

"Why, if he'd only taken all these yellow jackets all down to the creek, baptized them, and put their names in the membership book," I replied, "within two weeks they'd have left the church. It works for humans often enough, doesn't it?"

My dining companion laughed. But if one's going to risk being stung by yellow jackets or people, at least we can presume that the less painful, harmful kind will be more common this weekend. Happy Apple Days.

THE RUBAIYAT OF JOE AND KELLY

When I noted a couple of weeks ago that in years of working with both Christians and Muslims I'd only witnessed one open but friendly religious disagreement between the two faiths, I didn't mean I never knew ABOUT any other such quarrels. And there were a very few Muslims in eastern Kentucky well before the 1980s. From what I've heard, though, in the old days the most memorable conflicts locally occurred between only two men: my great-uncle Joe Meade, the town dentist of Inez many years ago, and a merchant in the same place, a Syrian pack-peddler or "drummer" who'd finally settled down to run a dry-goods store and who went by the name of Kelly Useem. Now, I don't know much about

Kelly Useem except that he was probably the sole Muslim in Martin County at that time, but Uncle Joe was—well, he was Uncle Joe. He kept an office in Inez but also carried a foot-operated dentist's drill to house calls, and when working on a patient he'd place two straight chairs back-to-back, have his patient sit in one, put his right foot up in the other, and use his right knee as a cushion for the patient's head as he drilled or yanked with all the skill the University of Louisville had given him between 1898 and 1902. He'd often drop by to ask my grandmother and my mother to boil his dental instruments, and on almost all these occasions he'd have a cache of pulled teeth with him, many of them, Dad swore, with more than a little gum tissue still clinging to them. I was too young to remember the teeth, although I doubt Dad and Mom would have let me look at them in the first place, but I don't think the old fellow ever charged much. I'm pretty sure that if a man offered to pay him in whiskey, or a woman by other means of barter, it was just fine with him. I inherited a typescript collection of poems he wrote, his

Scrabble board, a pack of his cards, and his dice, and I'll always remember him by all four—plus a passel of stories.

Uncle Joe, bless his heart, undoubtedly agreed more with his fellow poet Omar Khayyam than he did either Jesus or Muhammad, but for Kelly Useem if no one else he became a Christian apologist, more than likely simply for the sake of the argument. When he wasn't in his office or out on a call, like as not you'd find him at Kelly Useem's store, the two quarreling over the relative merits of Christianity and Islam. And in spite of the disagreement, I suspect both combatants enjoyed the fight and either would have been disappointed if the other had given it up.

They did get into trouble together at least once, though. Drinking with Uncle Joe was always a risky proposition. One time he and another friend got drunk together and he pulled all the friend's teeth. That strained the friendship—as well as the poor guy's food, afterward. But it so happened when I was a small boy, and Uncle Joe was well past eighty, that Kelly Useem got hold of a large saddle of mutton and whether or not Kelly observed his religion's ban on alcohol, both he and Uncle Joe ate themselves completely sick on mutton and Uncle Joe got dog-drunk besides. He managed to hitchhike from Inez to Williamsport, where he stumbled into the house of his youngest sister, my great-aunt Mae, and began to curse that mutton with a proficiency that rivaled his persuasive skill as a spiritual apologist to Kelly. As she'd done many times, Aunt Mae put him to bed until he sobered up. After he dried out he came to our house, from whence he visited a Paintsville physician and returned to us to take his cure. Don't ask. It involved a lot of mineral oil, in more than one place. When I reflect on how moody my mother often was, I try to remember that it was she who had to clean up after him that time, at my grandparents' insistence. And this was only one of his mishaps.

Uncle Joe's and Kelly Useem's long-gone day seems a time of innocence to us now, but it probably appears more pleasant through the rose-colored glasses of nostalgia than it really was. It would be nice, though, to see those who differ religiously get along as well as those two did, perhaps over a mutton dinner—but maybe with a little moderation, and minus the whiskey.

THE GOSPEL FIDDLER

It's a lot easier to be a church member than it used to be. Besides all the obvious luxuries—electric light and heat, indoor restrooms rather than spider-infested privies, thermos jugs or water fountains instead of wooden buckets and gourd dippers everybody had to share, and what not—there's a lot less anxiety to it. Back in the early days of settled eastern Kentucky there were only two denominations, Methodist and Baptist, and both could give their members a hard way to go. The idea of privacy was almost nonexistent. If you were a Methodist, the circuit rider expected to see you in "class" meeting, confessing your own particular sins before all your neighbors, outlining how you'd combated them, and promising to be a better person next time he visited. And Baptist churches used to have so-called Ruling Elders, whose job it was to examine yours and your family's conduct and report you to the church for "walking disorderly" as he saw fit. I'm not sure why the Baptists quit ordaining Ruling Elders. The office didn't inspire any affection, so maybe after Ruling Elders had torn up enough churches people recognized they were more harmful than beneficial. But whichever sect you attended, you better never get caught humming or singing any other tune than a hymn. And to dance to fiddle music—oh, Lord! The early central Kentucky Baptist preacher John Taylor wrote in 1822 that a good fiddler was the devil's right-hand man, and whenever any neighbors started hosting reels and square dances at their homes he just knew that Satan had set up camp right at his front door. After all, the devil himself was a fiddle player too; Charlie Daniels said so, and wrote a hit song about the old mountain tale in 1979.

No doubt many eastern Kentucky churches of old agreed completely with John Taylor, but strangely, that wasn't always the case in the territory that became Johnson and Martin Counties. One of the best known and best-loved frontier preachers between Tug River and the head of Paint Creek was the Paintsville pioneer Henry Dixon, who was not only a skilled fiddler but used his violin to gather crowds together for worship. According to the tales handed down locally, he'd attract listeners with several sprightly fiddle airs, then pray and preach, and finish up by sawing out a few more tunes—perhaps inducing his flock to sit through what could be a lengthy sermon for the sake of the music. At one time or another the old exhorter's pastorates included a place of worship on Rockcastle Creek in present Martin County, the churches now known as Old Union and Concord in Johnson, and another on the Open Fork of Paint Creek across the Morgan County line. And Dixon fiddled and preached between them all, and under his leadership the Rockcastle Church even acquired an old-fashioned bellowed pipe organ and had it transported up Tug River by flatboat. Agree with him or not, he was truly a man ahead of his time musically.

This isn't to say that Henry Dixon didn't endure his share of troubles. About 1826 an Ohio revivalist named Cleland came up the Big Sandy to Old Union to preach, boarding with Henry, his wife Joyce, and their family, and this visiting man of God wound up leaving three so-called "ruined girls" behind him, one of whom was Henry's daughter. Henry traveled north to confront the girls' seducer but wound up having to preach on Sunday at the 1826 session of the Ohio Baptist Association instead. For some reason he never caught up with Cleland, for which the revivalist probably should have been very thankful. But in any case, the good old preacher never held his grandson's parentage against him, raising the boy with his own children and letting him wear the Dixon name with pride.

Dixon died in 1854 at the age of eighty, and it's said that on his deathbed he called for his fiddle one last time and slowly played a hymn before passing on to a place of sweeter music. With all due respect to John Taylor, Henry Dixon was in no sense the devil's right-hand man. He was good to his parishioners and neighbors, and in that sense I'd like to think of him as the right-hand man to the angels instead. And who knows? Maybe Taylor's arguing about music with the old Gospel fiddler somewhere in eternity yet, as he reels off a lively tune—perhaps in duet with King David on the harp, and as the angels dance on the head of a pin.

HALLOWEEN, PART 1: CORN NIGHT

We're well into autumn now, and coming up on the holidays. Some stores have had their Halloween decorations out since before Labor Day, and by now they've already started to put up Christmas greens. But our very first forthcoming celebration is a longstanding tradition not only in eastern Kentucky, but the Midwest also and at one time, probably throughout the rural United States. October 30 is known in some places as Mischief Night, Goosey Night, and in parts of northern Kentucky as Cabbage Night, but around here it's always been Corn Night. And although the practice has declined a lot since I was young and perhaps even now it's honored more in the breach than the observance, there are still kids in eastern Kentucky who "go a-cornin'" on the night before Halloween.

I admit, Corn Night and Halloween are pagan in origin, and they go back in our history and our blood, long before there was a Church, to our British and German ancestors' harvest celebration that marked the beginning of the "darker half" of the year. In the olden days it was known among Celtic peoples as the festival of Samhain. Back in the era of the coal camps in eastern Kentucky the seasonal revelries could get very, very rough: even grownups would get into the act, blocking roads, setting fires, soaping windows, and tipping over outhouses. I personally know of one such case in which a woman was actually inside her privy when her neighbors toppled it, and later exacted retribution on them with the gift of a big batch of Ex-Lax brownies. They say revenge is like ice cream, best served cold, but at Halloween I suppose baked goods can work just as well. At least she didn't use razor blades. But needless to say, such escapades are the reason why in most areas of the country the first of the two Samhain-based holidays is called Mischief Night (and even Hell Night in Detroit), and in fact the grounds for its being known as Cabbage Night in northern Kentucky. There, the tradition seems to have been for pranksters to toss rotten cabbages onto the porches of houses. I guess that's better than setting a paper bag of feces alight at somebody's front door, yelling "Fire!" and then running, but those who have to get rid of decomposed cabbage the next morning might feel differently.

But the way Corn Night got its particular name around here actually speaks more of charity and goodwill than mischief. Samhain—and later, All Hallows' Eve or Halloween after the Church decided that November 1 and 2 were All Saints' and All Souls' Days, respectively—was always regarded in folk culture as a so-called "liminal" time, when for some reason the barriers between the Other World and this one could be breached more easily. This accounted for the belief in the presence of ghosts, goblins, fairies, and what not around the end of October, and along with it both the donning of costumes and the increase of mischief: people simply acted out their time-honored legends and, mostly with tongue in cheek, blamed the damage they did on the supernatural beings that were supposed to be out in force. But the source of the term Corn Night, the practice of tossing seed corn on the front porches of your neighbors, was different. According to the principles of old, the grain was actually an offering to the Otherworldly beings, a request to them to help themselves to the corn and leave the house in peace. Thus the presence of corn at your door was in fact both a friendly prank and an indication of respect, a sign that your neighbors and their children wished you well. Whether it's a pagan pre-Christian tradition or not, a goodwill gesture is never a bad idea.

      Soon we'll once again hear the annual dire proclamations about the so-called "war on Christmas" from the same forces who like to remind us that Corn Night and Halloween are sinful because they're pagan. How ironic: at one time in this country, the Puritan colonies of New England regarded Christmas itself as heathen, based more on the ancient Roman Saturnalia and German Yuletide festivals than on the birth of Jesus, and they'd lock up and fine anyone they found celebrating the day publicly. But I doubt we need to worry about the disappearance of any of our customary holidays any time soon. Maybe the issue simply depends on what side of the outhouse door one is on when it's tipped over. Stay safe on Corn Night, all.

HALLOWEEN, PART 2: HAINTS

I was about eleven when "The Exorcist" came out and probably fourteen or so when a censored version of it first aired on one of the three channels then available on television, and I can't recall a movie that caused more extreme responses among young people. I knew a set of sisters who were so frightened by it that after they watched it, for two or three weeks they insisted that their mother sleep with them. One guy old enough to drive told me he could sense the devil riding shotgun beside him when he left the old Sipp Theater after the show, but one or two others, brighter than most of us, would laugh all the way through the movie and watch it again and again for the tight hugs they always got from their terrified dates. Ah, those were the days. When "The Twilight Zone" and "The Outer Limits" were in regular syndicated reruns on those three channels and "Night Gallery" and "Ghost Story" were still on prime time, demons and ghosts and what not—what our grandparents, and sometimes our parents too, would call "haints" after the old pronunciation of "haunts"--could be a very grave business, no pun intended, of course all the more serious at this season of the year.

    I don't know how much my old man knew about child psychology, but the stories he told me about haints when I was a little kid somehow helped me cope with my fears in a way nothing else did. Back then I didn't know that Dad only believed in what he could see and about half of what he heard, but he sure could recall how a young boy's mind worked. Our home was an old coal company crackerbox built in 1902, just like those of most of our neighbors, and those houses had seen dozens of tenants over the years and a lot of births and deaths. So when I'd get scared about the possibility of ghosts roaming the place, Dad would simply say not to worry: likely they were only house haints, and house haints never caused trouble. They were quiet and wanted to be left alone. It was the field haints outside that were full of mischief, the kind that would throw things at you and try to trip you up. Dad's story about field haints may have been his plan to try to keep me indoors at night, and I guess it worked, but somehow his Linnaean classification of haints (backed up by Grandma, who believed in them a lot more literally than Dad ever did) served to make the ghosts, or at least a kid's fears, more manageable for me. Sort of like his story, when I was even younger, of "the tater wagon a-goin' up the road" when I'd be startled by loud thunder.

And of course I eventually learned the truth about haints: to quote Dad again, hain't none, really.

Maybe that's the function of myth in general, to help humans cope with what they don't understand until they're mature enough not to need the mythical explanations any more. There's a moral there, folks. But, that said, I must warn you that if you're looking for skeptics about the supernatural don't bother poking around a hospital staff. Many healthcare workers have college degrees in the applied sciences and there are individual rationalists among us, but collectively I never saw a more superstitious bunch in my life. Every patient care unit I've ever worked with harbors its own collection of eerie stories, my coworkers choose their words carefully to avoid jinxes, and once years ago when my union was on strike a gaggle of my college-educated professional colleagues traveled all the way to another county to ask a fortune teller when the labor dispute was going to end. The very laboratory where I now work is supposed to have a haint lurking somwhere in it, the ghost of a technologist who died in a car accident not too far from the hospital, and although some of my coworkers have sworn they've seen her—and we even have one instrument that's named for her—I've never seen or heard so much as a peep out of her, even around midnight. If she exists at all, I feel sorry for her. How much fun can it be to have to haunt a laboratory, of all places? Maybe I've simply scared the poor thing off, hopefully to better haunts. Pun intended this time.

Or like Dad used to say, perhaps she's just a quiet house haint who hain't no harm. Happy Halloween.

SHOUTIN' ON THE HILLS OF GLORY

Folks don't seem to be as openly emotional in church quite the way they used to be when I was a kid. I know, the practice of "rejoicing" has always been frowned upon by many town churches and at least one country denomination I could name, but for the most part it's been an accepted facet of religious worship around here ever since the first white settlers came in. I don't think that the present lack's caused by any extra or worse "sin," as some preachers I know have been accustomed to speculate. Sin's always been a favored hobby everywhere. The angriest sermon I ever heard preached on that particular subject came from a man who later got into trouble enough to make Jimmy Swaggart or Jim Bakker blush—or maybe to feel sorry for him instead. Customs, habits, and fashions simply change over time, and that's all there is to it. So as best as I can figure, the more or less fashionable method of "rejoicing" nowadays is to close your eyes, tilt your head upward, look as pious as you're able, and wave one arm back and forth over your head —or perhaps on an extra special Sunday, both arms although I get the impression that's a minority habit. Too many elbows can quench the Spirit, I imagine.

Even so, this whole modern demonstration can be performed quietly, without the main facet I remember from my youth: shouting. Sometimes that shouting could get loud, its accompanying physical actions could get extremely physical, and there's a sort of hilarious charm about the old-time way of doing things that mere eye-closing, arm-waving, head-tilting, and pious expressions just can't compete with. I more or less grew up under the preaching of Don Fraley on Boyd Branch, and when Preacher Don got excited and you happened to be sitting in or anywhere near the pulpit, you didn't merely get your face slapped; he'd play virtual tetherball with your head or, if you happened to be like Zacchaeus, short of stature, he'd do crack-the-whip with your entire little bitty self. In spite of Preacher Don's example, though, a younger exhorter (the same kid who wanted to sic Elisha's bears on an older colleague for criticizing his skipping school) once tried some of the same antics on me and I must confess it didn't work out quite so well for him. Imitation may be the sincerest form of flattery, but age hath its privileges. Youth doesn't-eth.

Physical demonstrations weren't limited to the preachers, of course. One old fellow I recall in particular would waltz you all the way from the back of the church to the front if he got happy enough, and one time he became so enthusiastic during a foot washing that he accidentally punched a woman right in the kidney, requiring her family to rush her from the church house to the emergency room. And this was only one of many such folks I've known. But the most dramatic case of this sort I ever saw was a neighbor who, for some reason, became determined to walk the backs of the pews during a shouting time. Now, if you've never seen that done, it's a sight to behold, and although I never felt any urge to try it myself I imagine that any practitioner of the pew-walking art must strike some sort of balance—no pun intended—between foot coordination, hand clapping, shouting, and any other accompanying expressions of joy he or she might attempt. Thus pew-walkers were held in very high esteem in some quarters, perhaps for a similar reason I once heard a deacon admiringly describe one of his favorite preachers: "When you hear him start to cluckin' like a hen, you know the Spirit's just all over him." In other words, when somebody climbed up on a pew back, you knew...well, you get the idea.

And so sure enough, one very happy Sunday night during a time of general rejoicing my old neighbor began to carry out his resolution. Climbing onto the back of the last pew on the left side of the church, he balanced precariously, then stepped to the next, then the next, and began to clap his hands above his head. His expression was rapt, as if he could see beyond the veil of this life through to the glory world, and then suddenly his feet slipped. One leg went down on one side of a pew, one on the other, the point of impact was directly in the middle...

And THEN he started shouting. Those were the days.

THE SHOULDERS OF GIANTS

It's Election Day, so let me try to be inspirational—that is to say, completely nonpolitical.

Recently a reader asked me where I came up with ideas for my column. Perhaps I did her a disservice by replying with my stock answer: "Aw, I just hear things here and there, and then it turns out I've been too lazy to forget 'em." She laughed, and the rejoinder seemed to satisfy her. Yet, even though there may be a lot of truth in the quip, I must admit that it wasn't quite original. I cribbed it from one of my favorite newspaper columnists of years gone by, the Louisville Courier-Journal's Joe Creason, who was himself very much a Common Tater at heart if not in name.

All this leads up to a great big tip of the hat to all of the writers that inspired, and still inspire, me. One of the cardinal rules all writers know is that if you're going to write, first you have to read, and you can't help but be influenced by what you see and absorb. And I've had the good fortune to have read and studied some fine Kentucky columnists in my time, some of whom I mentioned in my first Common Tater article. Besides "Joe Creason's Kentucky" there was Allen Trout and his "Greetings from Old Kentucky," the Frankfort editor Samuel Craig Van Curon with "Agree or Not, I Say What I Think" (I love that title, though I observe it myself a lot more on Facebook than I do in this milieu), and John Ed Pearce, whose columns needed no titles; his name on the byline was enough. And then, of course, there's the inimitable Red Dog, Larry Webster, who after thirty-odd years can still make almost the whole of eastern Kentucky mad—oftentimes simply because he makes them think. Plus a good many others, some of whom are still writing and whose publishers might not want their names mentioned in competing papers. Thus I know that, whatever new subjects and ideas I might introduce as the Common Tater, it's because I stand on the shoulders of giants.

But there is one local writer whom I've not yet mentioned, and I should have, because of all the columnists I've followed I think I miss her articles the most: Billie Edyth Ward of Boons Camp in Johnson County, whose "Back Then" feature was popular reading material throughout Johnson and Martin Counties in the 1980s into the early 1990s. Miss Ward was a career elementary school teacher, but after her retirement she worked just as hard on local historical and genealogical research as she had in her classroom. Like me, she believed that genealogy wasn't very interesting unless you had at least a few historical, human anecdotes to go along with the dry names on your pedigree chart, and in "Back Then" she spent a lot of time sharing such accounts with her eastern Kentucky neighbors. Our past as a people came alive in "Back Then," from traditional customs of midwifing all the way to the rites associated with the burial of the dead, with a lot of strong, not always good or nice, but often amusing personalities all along the road between—to which most of we Greasy Creek descendants were kin half a dozen different ways. "Back Then," to borrow her title, it was no different on any major watercourse in this county or most others surrounding it: only a few families settled on any of them, and after two or three generations all these clans were related from so many interweaving directions we can't genuinely say we have family trees so much as we have family wreaths.

Miss Ward's gone, and sadly, so are most of the living memories of "Back Then." We live in a world now in which younger people can hardly comprehend how we ever got along without microwave ovens and smart phones, let alone mere one-, two-, and three-channel television cable services. And while we don't, and cannot, know exactly what the future holds, I often wonder how many of the crafts and skills Miss Ward described so well in "Back Then" that future generations—and perhaps even our own—will one day have to re-learn simply in order to survive.

If this should happen, I hope we can resurrect and maintain the dry wit of Allen Trout and Joe Creason, the incisive, sardonic humor of Red Dog, and the political acumen of Samuel Craig Van Curon and John Ed Pearce too. We'll all need to stand on the shoulders of giants then.

IF YOU DON'T TALK ABOUT IT... (PART 1)

As I've hinted often in this column, my favorite hobby is local historical/genealogical research. My most frequent partner-in-crime in this effort is a lovely lady to whom I'm related east-Kentucky fashion, several different ways between only a few families, from the Left Fork of Two Mile originally but now living downstate. I just got back from the County Library, having tried to run down some information for her from microfilms of our local papers about a suicide that occurred in this county eighty-nine years ago. As I might have expected, I learned nothing whatsoever from the community news media. The two issues of the newspaper immediately after the date of the tragedy contained a number of remarkable articles including one about an individual who fell from a twelve-story building in New York City, and another claiming the Garden of Eden had been in America (this was the Roaring Twenties, after all, the Reagan Era on steroids)—but left a complete blank for a fifty-eight year-old farm wife, mother, and grandmother who, in a day and age when the United States was supposed to be God's Own Nation and Kentucky was where He was best worshiped, one early autumn morning decided that life just wasn't worth living anymore and ended her own by drowning. And now, as with the legendary Inconnue de la Seine, we'll never know her griefs or her motivation.

In modern Appalachia suicides are often written off conveniently and complacently as mentally ill and therefore probably not responsible for their actions, but years ago nearly everyone considered them as damned eternally. Back then too, a good many churches and ministers around here were known for a bit of self-righteous depravity called "preaching a man (or woman) into hell" at funeral services, much like the priest in Shakespeare's "Hamlet" did with Ophelia. This deplorable practice is, thankfully, almost nonexistent now—but because the Church has historically taught that suicides must either be hell-bound or unhinged, mostly the former, should this despondent grandmother's neighbors and kin have thus consigned her very memory to oblivion too, an idea seemingly scarier to most people even than hell is, and the possible lack of an afterlife more terrifying than the possible absence of a God? All that my downstate friend and I could do was shake our heads and recall a proverb that both of us had learned almost from the time we were able to talk, and which had been repeatedly drummed (literally) into us growing up: *IF YOU DON'T TALK ABOUT IT, IT NEVER HAPPENED.*

You rarely see anything written about Appalachia that isn't nostalgic. The Good Old Days, simpler times, country living, family closeness, what not: we've idealized ourselves almost beyond recognition, Waltonized our culture you might even say, and outsiders have often swallowed the deception hook, line, and sinker. If you don't believe me, read the early novels of Janice Holt Giles and then check out Diane Watkins Stuart's biography of her to see how differently she expressed herself in private after she moved to Kentucky. I'm not saying that our culture doesn't have qualities to admire and even emulate, but after having grown up in, out of, and then back into eastern Kentucky I know for a fact that the age-old mountain attitude of silence and cover-up for inconvenient truths as vital to a family's or a community's well-being isn't one of them. It's been used to hide sexual assaults, abuses, and scandals, depression and other mental disorders short of full-blown insanity that couldn't be concealed, addictions, overdoses, church politics and dissensions, and a host of other things that many of us natives have at one time or another been reminded by the back of an older hand across our young mouths never to dare bring up again. And about all it's succeeded in doing is to foster some very unhealthy coping mechanisms and a weird sense of humor in abuse survivors, which can often serve only to perpetuate the creed of mum's-the-word. Not to mention suicides, which are swept under the rug with the same complacent attitudes and platitudes again and again. Want to see eastern Kentucky improve? How about from the ground up, forsaking all the nostalgia long enough to try to accept ourselves honestly as humans, with all of the both good and bad that the effort entails?

I'll have something a little more upbeat in Part Two. If today's column has made you uneasy in any way, I guess you'll simply have to remain silent and pretend that I never wrote it. Remember: *IF YOU DON'T TALK ABOUT IT…*

IF YOU DON'T TALK ABOUT IT… (PART 2)

Since it's Thanksgiving week, I'll recall a memory for which I'm thankful. Among the many gifts my father left me was a number of songs he learned in his boyhood from his maternal grandfather and uncles. I guess you could call the tunes Appalachian Folk Music, but to me in my childhood they were simply the songs Dad sometimes sang, in his memorable bass growl, when we were by ourselves. I learned the ancient Irish murder ballad "Rose Anne Lee" from him long before I ever realized that the hymn "I'm a-Gonna Die on the Battlefield" had exactly the same tune. Interestingly, that old ditty was one of the cleaner pieces in Dad's repertoire. Another was about a man who came home one night to find a stranger's head on his pillow, which his wife insisted was a cabbage head although the husband had never seen a cabbage with a mustache before. Then the poor soul got confused similarly about a rolling pin. And there was still another that... nope. You'll have to wait to hear me sing it sometime in privacy. Strict privacy. I can't even put the title in a family newspaper. Mom never could stand it, and neither can Sweet Tater. But it's still durned funny.

I suppose you could say that our stalwart ancestors sought pleasure and amusement humbly, in a time and place that offered very little of either. But ribald music was only one evidence of their quest, and modern-day local historical investigation often finds itself checked by a heavy dose of our already cussed-and-discussed Appalachian maxim "if you don't talk about it, it never happened." Many of Dad's humorous songs centered around women outwitting men sexually, but real life was very much the man's world—and largely still is. Doing genealogical research I've found at least four male ancestors who hired "housekeepers" to assist ailing or invalid wives, started siring children on their new employees, and then married their "hired girls" after their wives passed away. And this all occurred in the eighteenth and nineteenth centuries, an era not only when people were supposed to be more godly and religious overall than they are in our own supposedly degenerate times, but when adultery was actually a legal offense, punishable by fine if not imprisonment! Add illegitimate births, shotgun weddings, sufferers from so-called "bad diseases," and one great-great aunt, a minister's wife, who died "trying to keep from having children" (I never dared ask what that meant), and I've got one interesting family tree.

Though males enjoyed their dalliances, females often didn't have that luxury. Poor women frequently had to assume the "housekeeper" role simply to avoid starvation. One of my ancestors was the orphaned teenaged sister of the son-in-law of an old Revolutionary veteran. I suppose her brother and sister-in-law got her the caretaker's job with the ex-militiaman, but I wonder what they must have thought over the next thirty-odd years as she bore him child after child—a couple before his wife's death and six or eight afterward. She finally married the old soldier after their children were grown, when she was fifty and he was eighty-four. Another instance was that of a destitute widow with a baby to feed; my great-great-great grandfather gave her five more after the two moved in with him and his wife. Still one more case was a girl driven from her parents' home for bringing the "shame" of an illegitimate grandchild on them, but who found another of my male ancestors to be more forgiving. And we can't forget the sad plight of the first wives, who were probably in ill health and in any case were unable to oppose the new household arrangements foisted upon them by their lusty husbands. I guess they all learned to get along someway, although I can't imagine how. And then there was my poor great-great aunt…

I can hear my mother and grandparents now: "John, must you write about this? Our people are respectable!" But any family tree has as much honor and distinction in it as dishonor, and after the latest Presidential campaign it's become obvious that both "honor" and "dishonor" are actually pretty nebulous terms in most people's minds. The only way we can ever really understand the present is to accept the past as it was, and that means being honest about both beauty marks and warts. It's better to seek the truth wherever you may find it, and if a little music helps the search, just hum along with the ballad about the man who lost his... err, never mind.

INTRODUCING CHUCK Q. FARLEY

I've reached a milestone in my journalistic career. George Washington Harris had Sut Lovingood, Mark Twain had Mr. McWilliams, Langston Hughes had Jesse B. Simple, "Red Dog" Webster's got Tie Rod, Jimmy Breslin has any number of people from the streets of New York

City, and finally I've snared one myself: a valuable resource person who doesn't mind being quoted in my column. So I'd like to take this opportunity to introduce my readers to Charles Quinlan Farley. Or Chuck Q. Farley, as he seems to prefer it for some reason.

I wouldn't call Chuck Q. a fan so much as a worthy adversary. I like him well enough and he claims he likes me, but when I published "The Reign of King Mob" last spring he Facebook messaged me, threatening to rock my windows like Ernest T. Bass after the November election for condemning our patriotic forefathers who voted Andrew Jackson into office to set our people free. He renewed the threat after my "Pulpit Politics" series for my criticism of God's Anointed, who he felt must never be touched. But since the election's over, my windows are still intact, and he blocked me on Facebook, I figured I at least owed him a phone call to hear what had changed his mind. Apparently it was either the election itself, or a change of heart on his part. Or maybe both.

"Aw, Drackler," he said, using his favorite nickname for me, "since the election turned out okay and everybody's goin' back to work now, you couldn't of done no harm to it. And besides, nobody much ever reads nothin' no way, so rockin' your windows wouldn't do no good. But I seen the error of my ways and got right since the last time you and me talked. So now I'm just gonna warn you about your wicked writin' before Jesus Hisself rocks your windows for you at the Judgment, praise God!"

"Well, Mr. Farley," I attempted to answer, "Um... would it be okay if I called you Charley?"

"No!" he snapped. "Charley Farley? That's plumb ignorant! You persecutin' me? I'm Chuck Q. Farley!"

"I understand, Chuck Q.," I replied. "Just don't ask me to repeat your name several times fast. So you say your candidate won, and now you're going back to work?"

"Wasn't just MY candidate, it was God's too," he countered. "All the preachers said so, and how could that many of 'em be WRONG? But work… well, you see, I *RESPECT* work. I respect it every bit as much as I do my own dear sweet old mother. In fact, I respect both work and my mother so much that I've never struck either one of 'em a lick in my entire life. But my neighbors that ain't workin', them that wants to work, anyhow, surely some of *THEM'll* go back to work."

"Well, Chuck Q., downstate where I work on weekends, if the new President gets his way there'll be a lot of farm jobs open. Good hard labor too, out in the sun where you'd get lots of Vitamin D. Maybe you should ride down with me and talk to some of the farmers and get your foot in the door for early planting. Tobacco's a nearly year-round crop. They raise horses and cattle too, and they'll need workers."

I could hear him snort through the phone. "*FARM* work? Too hard for too little! Let them people stay where they is!"

"But since your candidate won the election, and you voted for him and his program—"

"I did not!" he exclaimed. "Vote? Me? If I registered to vote I could get called up for jury duty, and I hain't about to set on no jury, no more'n I'd join the Army!"

Then the truth came to me: he was right. With that lifelong attitude, how could he vote, sit on a jury, serve in the military, or do anything with tobacco besides smoke and chew and dip it? So I had to tip my hat to him, because he had thoroughly out-argued me. That's when I asked him if I could use him as a resource person for my Common Tater column, and he agreed, vowing to point me back to the Strait and Narrow Path yet. He Facebook friended me again, too. For all this I thanked him.

So from now on, when I get stumped on an issue I'll ask Chuck Q. Farley about it and share his wisdom with you. Next week I'll tell you how I first met him. And why he calls me Drackler.

EARLY TIMES & TOENAILS

Last week I promised I'd tell you how I met my journalistic guide and counselor, Chuck Q. Farley. I didn't call him by that name at first, though. We were both a lot younger then, and that night I could identify him only by his Intensive Care Unit armband, *"FARLEY, CHARLES QUINLAN, ICU 812."* He was a direct admit from the Emergency Room, having been discovered passed out drunk face-down in mud somewhere and almost frozen to death, and he had more dirt in his eyes than I thought was even possible. (A note here: I got Chuck Q.'s permission to tell this, as well as that of Dr. Skinnerbach, the physician on call that night. Both agreed, Chuck Q. because his wife thought his example might do some good if made public, and Dr. Skinnerbach because he'd completely forgotten the case and was interested.) And of course I was summoned to draw blood. I introduced myself; then and for years after, I addressed Chuck Q. only as Mr. Farley, and he called me—well, never mind what he called all of us, especially the nurse trying to clean him up after Dr. Skinnerbach rinsed the dirt out of his eyes with a squirt bottle of warmed sterile saline.

"Be careful, Mr. Farley," I whispered as the nurse momentarily left the ICU cubicle. "One time a guy in here kicked her, and she took revenge by cleaning under his toenails with the sharp point of a great big pair of scissors. Went to the quick and brought out stuff that hadn't seen daylight in years. I watched it happen."

He paled and curled up his toes tightly. "Thanks, buddy," he whispered, and abruptly became all honey, pie, and charm to the returning nurse. Then he addressed me again. "You a vampire?" he chuckled.

That joke was funny the first time I heard it. Not so much the million since. "No, sir," I replied, straight-faced, "I'm a tick, and my wife and kids are mosquitoes." He laughed, but refused to let me draw any blood.

"Buddy, I got blood tests done just yesterday at the doctor's, and I don't think I need no more this soon," he explained. That was enough for me, so I turned to leave. It was his right to refuse a venipuncture. But then the nurse tried to coax him into it.

"Hold on a minute, John," she ordered. "Mr. Farley," she begged, "we need to know how much alcohol you have in your blood."

"Honey—err, Nurse, Ma'am, I don't mean you no disrespect, but I can tell you that. They's a fifth of Early Times in there. Or maybe Seagram's Seven. I forget. Just leave my toenails alone, okay?" He looked at her worriedly.

"Toenails?" she asked, her eyes darting suspiciously towards me. "What about toenails?" I gave her a scatophagic grin. She glared back at me.

Dr. Skinnerbach entered the cubicle, evidently having overheard our conversation. "Mr. Farley," he said politely, with the bare hint of German accent that still clings to his excellent English, "Besides caring for your eyes, I must know your blood alcohol level."

"I done told her, Doc, they's a *FIFTH* in there!"

"But...but...," the good doctor sought for an explanation, "I still need to ascertain the concentration. Otherwise, if we give you anything for pain or anxiety tonight, it might knock you completely out!"

Chuck Q. looked aggrieved. "But that's what I *WANT!*" he wailed plaintively. I bit my lip to suppress a smile. You have to admire honesty wherever you find it.

The nurse started to offer a comment. "Dr. Skinnerbach—" she began.

Chuck Q. did a violent double-take and stared at her in abject terror. "No, no, not that!" he howled as he sowbugged himself into a fetal position. "Go ahead, Count Drackler, draw the blood," he sobbed, holding out one arm, "but PLEASE don't nobody do that! Nor jam nothin' up nowhere afterwards! And for God's sake leave my toenails alone too!"

The nurse scowled at me again, and Dr. Skinnerbach just looked puzzled. I did manage, however, to collect a sample of Chuck Q.'s blood, and he even complimented me on my technique. After he recovered he asked the nurse out on a date, she agreed, and they wound up getting married and moving downriver a few miles. Her name's Polly Esther, by the way, and although she never could make Chuck Q. work, she did persuade him to quit drinking and to keep his toenails nice and clean for her. Both worthy ideas, if he knows what's good for him.

A MODEST PROPOSAL

I've been hearing a lot locally since the Presidential election about flag burning. It's certainly a hot-button issue with emotions running high on at least one side, but I can't help being somewhat perplexed. Eastern Kentucky seems to me to be one of the least likely places in the world where one might witness the burning of an American flag. The only regional tale I've ever heard of such, and it's apocryphal at best, comes from nearly one hundred years ago when a small group of Communists were supposed to have attempted a rally not long after the end of World War I at some mountain county seat or other. After the local citizens' response to their flag fire the Communists were apparently very glad to get out of the hills with their skins. In short, even though we are now told that a certain former KGB officer is actually the United States' bestest buddy ever, and for the time being people are apparently swallowing the notion hook, line, and sinker, flag burning is still something that just ain't done in eastern Kentucky. For which I'm very glad. It's not only in poor taste, it's stupid.

But admittedly, whether it's right or wrong, the main reason that the act is so easy to condemn around here may be that flag burners are completely safe to hate, since almost none of us have brothers or sisters or cousins or any other kinfolk guilty of the practice. I guess the religious equivalent in terms of community consensus would be something like the issues of gayness versus divorce and remarriage. Gays are decidedly in the minority and therefore currently very easy to condemn, whereas divorce has become accepted a lot like the television set once was—when enough people got one, at least within the families of ministers, the churches pretty much quit quoting Scripture about it and preaching against it. And so the flag-burning issue remains alive and agitated locally, not least because our President-elect has recently "tweeted" the proposition that flag burners ought either to lose their citizenship or be jailed—while our state's own Senior Senator, Mitch McConnell, vocally upholds the 1989 Supreme Court ruling that flag burning is an issue of Freedom of Speech and therefore a legitimate form of political protest. I won't attempt to step in between the two on the issue. For the President-elect's idea to be enacted, current Federal law would have to be changed, and if you don't like McConnell's opinion on the matter I suggest that you vote against him next time he runs, or for that matter, vote FOR him if you agree with him. What I'd like to leave with you is the idea that there's a much better and more legitimate form of political protest available than the incineration of the Stars and Stripes. That is, at least as long as you don't live in South Carolina, Georgia, Florida, Mississippi or Louisiana.

Simply put, why burn the American flag when you can light up a Confederate battle flag instead? Though "the Stars and Bars" is widely touted as some sort of beloved historical symbol, and in fact a great many of my own ancestors no doubt felt affection for it back when they fought under it, the Confederate flag isn't the official emblem of any legitimate nation. However much the Civil War is romanticized now, all the Secessionist banner ever really stood for was organized rebellion, spearheaded by a rich planter class leading a great many simple, well-meaning small farmers gulled by the planters' empty promises (like my forefathers were), against the lawful government of the United States. And I suspect that, even now, the Confederate flag remains a more potent symbol of everything worthy of protest against the wrongs and injustices of the American nation than the Stars and Stripes ever could be. In the five states listed above, the burning of a Confederate flag is illegal, but even in those the anti-burn law would be even more difficult to enforce than any similar prohibition against the destruction of the Stars and Stripes. That's not to say, though, that a Confederate flag-burner wouldn't run the same risk in, say, a rural Georgia or Florida panhandle county seat that the Communists once did with our own hill people over our true flag.

But we're not in those states. We're in Kentucky, and there's no Confederacy any more. Only the United States. May we always remember that, especially since, only four short years ago, people from many Southern states, including several thousand in this one, were actually petitioning once again to secede.

THE DAYS WERE ACCOMPLISHED

Much of my life as a hospital worker, and once upon a time as a nonsalaried country preacher trying to earn a living as a hospital worker, has involved my attempts to process and understand the things I've experienced—to make sense out of them as they related to my own life and to life in general. Thus, writing has become a vocation for me, and I admit that between fiction and nonfiction I've often had to pen some pretty dark, sordid stuff: sicknesses and deaths of children and adults both, loss of faith and hope, the disastrous, childish concept of a god who looks like a thinner, taller version of Santa Claus and behaves as if he were a superhero wearing a toga rather than tights and a cape. Write what you know, they say, and a good deal of my impetus seems always to have come from faith, doubt, rural churches, and rural hospitals in equal measure. And so for Christmas, let me share an experience much in my thoughts at this season.

We all wondered why the girl had come to our Emergency Room so early that cold morning. Her obstetrician worked at a larger hospital several miles upriver and ours was just a little place, twenty-odd patient beds and an obstetrics department that had been closed for years. As St. Luke once phrased it, there simply wasn't any room in the inn.

But for whatever reason, here she was in the ER, a frightened teenaged girl along with her frightened teenaged husband. And again as St. Luke phrased it, the days were accomplished that she should be delivered, and she was going to have that baby whether or not any of us wished that she would get an ambulance to take her somewhere else—or even wait till daylight to give birth.

If everything hadn't been so tense it would have been the stuff of comedy. A semi-retired gynecologist lived just up the hill from the hospital. She was roused from sleep and, luckily for the reluctant, equally rudely-awakened ER physician, proved willing to bestir herself and exercise her obstetrical skills one more time. Tools and materials packed up and gone into disuse ever since our own OB department had closed were frantically sought and finally found, amid laughter, tears, collisions, curses, and prayers of both supplication and thanksgiving. The House Supervisor barked orders in a tone that would have seemed absolutely furious if we all hadn't known it was the result of her genuine worry for the welfare of the girl.

And so in the wee hours of that icy morning, the baby was safely "caught." We were all prepared for the worst: stillbirth, breach birth, apnea, placenta praevia, placental abruption, umbilical cord around the throat, spina bifida, all the horrible things we knew that could occur; but the child was as healthy as a little colt, and was kicking almost as hard. The ER looked literally as if a tornado had passed directly through it, and the young father, dazed and seemingly wobblier on his legs even than the newborn, had to beg half a dozen smiling, cooing nurses for a brief turn at holding his own baby girl.

No one on duty that morning would have considered such a case, in the abstract, as being anything less than a nightmare come true. But in reality, that emergency delivery put every one of us in a good, even joyous, mood.

There are a couple of stories in the Bible about shepherds and wise men journeying to a stable outside an inn to visit a newborn. I admit, I've seen much in my occupation that would challenge the claim that either of those tales is relevant to life as it is today. And even on the assumption, or the faith, or the trust, or the hope, or the whatever, that the stories ARE relevant,

Scripture doesn't mention a single thing about any stable hands running around to help Mary and Joseph with the baby or anything else. But a happy birth still lets me catch a tiny glimpse of the Divine and makes me want to meditate on the old stories. And I'd like to think that a few stable hands WERE there in Bethlehem to wipe the brow of another, long-ago teenaged mother sweating and crying in the cold, each angling for a chance to hold and rock the baby and smiling with joy that a new life was born into the world. The divinity of birth is one of the things that keeps us hospital folk going, after all.

Merry Christmas.

NEW YEAR'S CABBAGE

Within the past three months we've been through three sets of quasi-religious holidays with more or less pagan origins. Corn Night and Halloween were both established Celtic traditions long before the Church declared November 1 to be All Saints' Day, Thanksgiving coincides with

England's ancient harvest celebrations, and of course Christmas was the Winter Solstice festival in many ancient cultures thousands of years earlier than the birth of Jesus of Nazareth ever became associated with the date. And so now, as a sort of goodbye to 2016 and a welcome to 2017, many eastern Kentucky families will be ringing in the New Year with one more time-honored custom with origins in ancient superstition: the cooking and eating of cabbage on January 1, which is supposed to assure good luck and prosperity for an observant household in the coming year. You can use plain boiled cabbage of the type you serve up with corned beef and pinto beans, sauerkraut if you prefer it to the fresh article, cabbage rolls if you want to make it a little bit fancier, even egg rolls or kimchi if you're into Asian cuisine; as long as some form of cabbage is in your New Year's Day meal, good luck is supposed to be there as well.

My folks weren't superstitious about most things, so I'm not sure why they insisted on following the cabbage tradition. Maybe the fact that their parents also observed it was enough to continue it from year to year. At least that's Sweet Tater's rationale for maintaining it, and I suppose it's as good as any. For whatever reason, back when I was young it was always boiled cabbage on January 1 at my folks', and my mother used to put a dime in the pot when she cooked it, I assume to bring extra luck to whomever found the coin on his or her plate when dinner was dished up. Dad always preferred, or at least claimed to prefer, the inclusion of a rusty horseshoe instead of a dime, but Mom never was willing to serve up a meal fortified with quite that much iron. An old horseshoe was good enough to nail up over the top door post (always with the argument, too, about whether the ends should be pointing upward to catch good luck or downward to distribute it, and whether or not the ends pointing down brought bad luck instead of good) but not for the cabbage pot.

All this leaves me wondering why we even bother with our old good-luck rituals. Are they, as Shakespeare's Hamlet phrased it, honored more in the breach than in the observance? As long as they're not taken too literally, they don't do any real harm, but then again they don't often do much good either. Maybe the traditions are worth observing simply to remember something of how our ancestors thought and acted. And there are actually a few old wives' tales, associated with the treatment of sickness at least, that make genuine medical sense. One of these is the maxim that "scorched things heal," and in a very real way, they do. Midwives used to scorch cloths over the fire to tie off umbilical cords and to swaddle newborn babies, without ever knowing that the real healing property of scorching was that heat sterilized the articles. Another, harking back to the idea that horseshoes bring good luck, was a remedy for iron deficiency that called for dissolving the metallic scraps or "clinkers" from a blacksmith's forge in vinegar, and then drinking the mixture as a tonic. My grandfather Sparks, who knew his way around both a blacksmith's shop and the motor barn of a coal mine in equal measure, used to swear by that one, and in fact it did provide a simple, homemade means for the relief of anemia long before over-the-counter vitamins had ever been dreamed up. I doubt that I'll ever get enough courage to taste that kind of concoction myself, though. To borrow another of Granddad Sparks' sayings, I just imagine it was sour enough to make a pig squeal.

In the end, I suppose that New Year's luck and traditions are questions I'll just have to take up with Chuck Q. Farley the next time I talk to him. He and Polly Esther have invited me and Sweet Tater down to eat cabbage with them on New Year's Day, and I anticipate that we'll have a lot to discuss and even a few things simply to cuss, or at least cuss at. So Happy New Year from our houses to yours—and enjoy your cabbage.

IM-TATERMENT

"Chuck Q., I'm fresh out of ideas for a new column," I said to my friend Chuck Q. Farley as we lingered at the table over coffee on New Year's Day. Our wives evidently preferred washing the dishes to listening to us. "Can you help me?"

"Well, it bein' New Year, what about the feller that stuck the pistol down his britches and got the trigger hung in his belt buckle?" he offered.

"That happened at midnight one New Year, sure enough, but I'm not certain I should write about it. Too much like John Bobbitt. But I guess I could use that story in another column about gun control."

"Drackler, don't be radical, now," urged Chuck Q. "I'm tryin' to cure you from writin' stuff like that. I've got another idear. How about the new President's impeachment?"

I blinked my eyes a couple of times. "What?" I asked. "Chuck Q., I thought you liked him!"

"Oh, he'll be great!" Chuck Q. enthused. "But I seen a bunch of stuff on the Internet claimin' he ort to be impeached, and I think he should at least try it out. Could be good for him. Can't hurt to see if it works."

"All right. Tell me how the new President would benefit from impeachment. This, I've *GOT* to hear," I sighed as I pushed my glasses up on my forehead and rubbed my eyes.

"Well, it's simple, Drackler. The man's good, but he ain't perfect, and you gotta admit, that orange makeup looks pretty stupid."

"Amen to that, but how—"

"Hear me out. So, let him just *TRY* peach makeup on instead of orange, and he might do better. First I thought he could get some of them pretty lady cosmetic stars on the home shoppin' networks to impeach him with it, maybe on live TV like that 'Makeover Story' reality show except it'll be on prime time, and them girls bein' experts with all colors, I'm sure they'd do a great job. There's two troubles I see, though. One, if he's impeached, peach makeup might make him look like he's got the yaller janders even more than he does already with that Eau de Sunkist—"

"Oh, Lord!" I groaned.

"And second, if he's on live TV, 'specially prime time, he'll have to resist the temptation to reach in and grab them cosmetic ladies by their—"

"Okay, okay, I get the point! Shh! Keep your voice down!"

"So you see, that could be a real deal breaker," he continued, unfazed. "Then I thought: why not use *MALE* makeup people instead, if need be? Now, I don't know any such men except undertakers. But I guess undertakers could work on a live person's face just as well as one of their ordinary customers, couldn't they?"

By now I was just rolling with the flow. "Well," I mused, "undertakers don't get the complaints from their ordinary customers that they would from live ones. Especially live Presidents with Twitter accounts. But since undertakers are always the very last people to let you down—yeah, why not use 'em?"

"Glad you agree, Drackler! So I'm gonna write the new President a letter. If I mail it tomorrow it should reach him before he's swore into office. I'll tell him that he ort to be impeached as soon as possible, and if he can't keep his hands to hisself, then undertakers needs to work on him!"

It took me a moment to respond to that one. I had to pick my jaw up off the floor, after all. "Chuck Q.," I finally said slowly and carefully, "If Polly Esther's got the good sense I remember her having when we worked together, she'll never let you mail that letter. The Secret Service could take it as a threat against the new President's person, or even his life! You'd make the national news, and have Men in Black all up and down the holler here! And get Twittered to death besides!"

"WHAT?" he exclaimed indignantly. "All that, just for me sharin' my good idears with the new President? I swear, people away from here can be *SO* stupid about things sometimes! Well... if you think it'd put me and Polly Esther and the kids in danger from them Twitter people, I won't do it, Drackler. But I wish I could come up with a colyum for you, at least."

"Don't worry, Chuck Q.," I replied as I wondered if the new President would ever know, or Tweet, about my secret good-faith effort in behalf of his peace of mind—as well as that of his Twitter followers. "You have."

HEAR THE ROYAL PROCLAMATION

Governor Bevin has proclaimed 2017 to be "The Year of the Bible" in Kentucky, although he did the same thing in December 2015 for the year 2016 and few Kentuckians took notice of it for more than a week. The announcement pretty much coincided, also for the second year in a row, with the so-called Kentucky 120 United Bible Reading Marathon, an event staged by a group called the Kentucky Prayer Focus and which involves volunteers statewide taking turns reading Scripture aloud until they orally complete the entire sixty-six books. I'm unsure what this is supposed to accomplish. Do the Governor and the Kentucky Prayer Focus think that this yearly ceremonial reading serves as some sort of annual gesture or invocation for God's blessing on the state? And if they do, wouldn't simple, silent prayers to that effect do more good? After all, Jesus of Nazareth once reasoned that God preferred private prayers spoken quietly from inside one's closet, and he gave a name to those who prayed out loud at the street corners for no other reason than that they wanted to be seen and heard: hypocrites. A little hypocrisy never stopped a politician—or the occasional football player—from making a grand gesture, though.

Still, even if it's politics as usual, I guess Bevin's and Kentucky's Year of the Bible is harmless enough. It's certainly preferable to what the State Legislature once did, proclaiming April 1986 as Jimmy Swaggart Month only a few months before the famous evangelist got caught with his britches down the first time. The real tragedy, I think, is that both The Year of the Bible and the Kentucky 120 United Bible Reading Marathon only emphasize what's already obvious: the Bible is the most-bought and most-praised, yet least-read and most-misread volume ever compiled in the history of the world. Saddest of all to me is how completely it's neglected within the United States as one of the very pillars, alongside Shakespeare's plays, of modern English language and literature. An entire generation, probably more than one, has grown up never having learned about the source of many common expressions they've heard all their lives: "the blind leading the blind," "forbidden fruit," "a little bird told me," "a leopard can't change its spots," "the left hand doesn't know what the right hand is doing," "a wolf in sheep's clothing," and a host of others originating in Scripture—including even the old song about the bones being connected together. And there's seemingly no way of fixing the problem, either within our present public school system or the quasi-religious setup which Governor Bevin and his cronies seem to want to replace it with.

All too often it's the case that the more observant you are religiously, the more heaven and earth hangs on doctrine and the more you quarrel over dogmatic questions. If the Bible were studied in elementary, middle, and high school in an academic fashion, like most other ancient writings are when they are studied at all, soon enough you'd have irate parents complaining that the course work somehow didn't give proper respect to a book that they regard as holy. Around here at least they'd likely perceive any comparison and contrast of the good old King James Version with later translations, or even the Hebrew and Koine Greek of the original writings, as introducing doubt and heresy to their children. And the same principle applies even if the Bible were taught from a doctrinal perspective, because there's so blasted much dogmatic disagreement. Immerse, pour, or sprinkle? Confession, penance, and absolution, or the "priesthood of all believers"? Musical instruments or just voices? Can you backslide, or are you heaven-bought and heaven-bound no matter what you do or say? Purgatory or simply split hell wide open? You can find justification for all in Scripture. Back when Christianity was newly recognized as the Roman Empire's state religion, there were street fights and actual killings in several cities over a dispute about the nature of Jesus of Nazareth—and ironically, in the Koine Greek then spoken throughout the Empire, the difference amounted to no more than one letter in one word. With a historical record like that, maybe we ought to regard religion like Chuck

Q. Farley respects both work and his mother: so much that he's never struck either one of them a lick in his entire life. Actually this may be exactly how Governor Bevin and most other politicians do respect religion. But it's not really a satisfactory solution, either.

The Year of the Bible? I'll never live to see the real thing. But I keep wishing.

POLITICS, PASTORING, & PEANUTS

"Well, Drackler, you made a nice column two weeks ago from my political idears. Real good work there," Chuck Q. Farley grumbled the next time we talked on the phone.

"It all made for a good story, Chuck Q.," I answered. "Politics makes the world go round, and if you and I can make people think even a little bit, we're doing our job."

He humphed. "Atter that Twitter danger, I've quit foolin' with politics. From now on I'm just gonna watch church programs and stay away from the news!"

"Well, if you can catch the address for that TV Miracle Water, send away for some and share it with me. But TV or not, you've always got to think politics in church too. The preachers and deacons do, anyway. Especially the pastor. And sometimes, everybody."

"Why you say that? You study Political Science along with all them other sciences you took, Drackler?" he asked.

"Never had a Political Science course in my life. I learned politics the hard way, right behind a pulpit."

He clicked his tongue. "That's right. You was once a preacher. Well, then, tell me why they has to be politics and politicians in church! If I'm gonna help you any more with that colyum, Drackler, I've gotta know somethin' about what you think."

"True enough," I admitted, and deliberated a moment. "Tell you what, Chuck Q. Once there was a fellow named Socrates who answered questions WITH questions, but he still got his points across. Years ago a really good teacher, rest her soul, showed me how to do it too. So let me try to answer you like Socrates. First question: how important is it in your religion to love your enemies, return good for evil, pray for those who mistreat you, turn the other cheek to somebody that hits you, that kind of thing?"

"Why, that's ever'thing that matters!" he shot back. "Well, doctrine, too, I guess..."

"Let's just let doctrine take care of itself for the time being. Second question: if all those things I mentioned are so important to your religion, where do you find that you have to use them the most? With 'sinner' people, or when you deal with your fellow church members?"

He pondered the query a moment, and grew solemn. "I never thought of it like that," he finally replied. "I'm gonna have to study on that one..."

"Well, study on this, too," I responded. "Third question: don't you think anybody having to lead a bunch that acts like that had better learn his politics fast, or else he'll have to soak 'em up through the knots he'll get on his head?"

Chuck Q. was silent. "Drackler, is that how come you quit preachin' and pastorin'?" he eventually asked quietly. "It wasn't no woman, like with so many?"

"No, no woman," I answered with a sigh, "though I halfway expected somebody would start up a rumor like that, even so." The phone was silent as I pondered. Had I already said too much, or not enough? There was no way for me to tell. Could anyone who hadn't actually been there truly under-stand mere words? I owed Chuck Q. some response, though, and so I took a deep breath and began to speak.

"Once I had a church member in the hospital, and I went to see him," I said. "We had a good visit, but he had a bowl of peanuts on his side table, and as we talked I'd reach over and grab a few peanuts and eat 'em. And finally I noticed that I'd absentmindedly eaten his entire bowl of peanuts.

"That really embarrassed me, so I apologized to him for eating all his peanuts and I promised him I'd go buy him some more right then. But he just looked at me with a great big gummy smile—poor old fellow didn't have a tooth in his head, you see—and he said to me, 'Brother John, it's okay. All I could do was lick the chocolate off them things, so you was welcome to the rest.'

"It never was the same after that," I concluded.

There was another moment of dead air on the phone, and then a snort. "Aw, shoot, Drackler," Chuck Q. complained, "You had me a-goin' there a minute. Shame on you! I nearly swallered that one whole! And now you've done gone and took my appetite too," he added reproachfully.

"Sorry, Chuck Q.," I answered, "let's just call that tale a parable. But if you had swallowed it whole, at least I hadn't licked off the chocolate first!"

FAKE NEWS & THE FILLMORE BATHTUB

We've heard a lot lately about fake news, and I suspect that before long we'll be hearing, and hearing about, a lot more. Sadly, dishonest journalism is actually a time-honored American institution. Thus far anyway, newspapers and other media outlets in the United States have been censored by the Government only during periods of outright war, and so for most of our history—during peacetime at least—the only way anyone could piece together a complete picture on any controversial subject was to buy and read three or four newspapers of varying political slants. After the end of World War II the Federal Communications Commission attempted to impose some reason and balance on the journalistic process by introducing and enforcing the so-called Fairness Doctrine, requiring media outlets to give print and air time to differing opinions about political controversies, and for as long as it lasted the Fairness Doctrine worked well. The FCC abolished it in the mid-eighties due to conservative pressure and Congress then attempted to codify its precepts as law, but Ronald Reagan vetoed the effort. Since then, journalism has gradually devolved to the Wild West Show that we know today, all in the name of Free Speech. If everyone had the presence of mind to check several newspapers and networks before trying to form an opinion of his or her own, things might not be so bad, but the prevailing ethic nowadays seems to be simply to believe whatever you want to; it's all legitimate.

In times like these we would do well to keep in mind the greatest literary hoax ever perpetrated in the history of American journalism: "A Neglected Anniversary," newspaper writer H. L. Mencken's spurious history of the bathtub, published initially within the heavy censorship confines of World War I. Mencken's essay first appeared in a New York City paper on December 28, 1917, claiming that the first American bathtub had been installed in a home in Cincinnati, Ohio in 1842 by a man who had traveled widely in Europe and had acquired the habit of regular bathing there. The event was supposed to have sparked widespread argument against bathing, with politicians claiming that the bathtub was a decadent European invention that had no place in republican America and physicians warning that washing might give a careless bather all manner of fatal diseases. In early 1851 the bathtub's cause was supposed to have been saved, however, by the thirteenth President of the United States. Millard Fillmore—and what better name for a bathtub supporter than that?—visited Cincinnati, took a bath in the historic pioneer tub, and then had one installed in the White House. After Fillmore's brave and progressive example, regular tub bathing caught on in the United States.

Not even Mencken himself could have anticipated the readiness with which the public swallowed his cock-and-bull story. It was printed, reprinted, quoted, and taken for law and Gospel by virtually everyone who read or heard of it. Within a few years' time it had even worked its way into legitimate history books, no one seemingly ever pausing to consider how utterly ridiculous the tale really was. Eight years after Mencken first published the piece he confessed his hoax and claimed that it had only been a joke, but it's suspected that he wrote it for a more serious purpose: to see just how far he could go in making the American public believe and perpetuate a baldfaced lie. And since the story continued to circulate for decades even after his retraction, and is in fact still quoted by some sources as truth, it's hard to say whether he was more amused, or more disgusted, by the results of his experiment.

H. L. Mencken was such an outspoken, pessimistic critic of human nature that he made a lot of enemies, particularly in the Bible Belt. The Arkansas legislature actually once passed a resolution to pray for his soul, although the legislators introduced the measure only after they learned that they couldn't force the Federal Government to deport him to Germany. His crimes? Such literary gems as this, written during Warren G. Harding's Presidential campaign in 1920: "As democracy is perfected, the office of president represents, more and more closely, the inner soul of the people. On some great and glorious day the plain folks of the land will reach their heart's desire at last and the White House will be adorned by a downright moron."

I suppose that, if this were ever to happen, we must hope that the leader in question should at least have a smarter daughter and son-in-law.

GROUNDHOGS, GERMANS, & GRANDFATHERS

We've practically made it through January now, and have only a short time of winter to look forward to—that is, if the groundhog doesn't see its shadow on February 2. Here's another holiday that had its origins in pagan times, marking the midpoint between the winter solstice and the beginning of spring and known originally known among the Celts as Imbolc. The Church renamed the day Candlemas as the occasion for the clergy to bless and distribute candles to their parishioners to help them through the remaining dark of winter, just as it made Christmas out of Saturnalia and Yule. (Christmas is, after all an abbreviation for "Christ Mass" just like Candlemas is for "Candle Mass." Thus, if you want to keep Christ in Christmas you should be equally enthusiastic about keeping the Mass in it, too. Just sayin'.) But at any rate, the first version of the Candlemas/Groundhog Day myth held that, if the weather was fair and sunny on Candlemas Day, six more weeks of harsh weather could be expected. If it was cloudy and cold, the winter weather would break sooner. As our ancestors once could say by rote: "If Candlemas be fair and bright, winter has another flight; if Candlemas bring clouds and rain, winter will not come again."

And again just like Christmas and Halloween, after the Reformation the celebration became secularized. The Germans first introduced an animal to the proceedings. Longstanding German tradition held that the perfect gauge for the weather on Candlemas Day was the badger. If it cast a shadow on February 2, a six-week cold, wet spell was assured afterward. German immigrants, not being able to find as many badgers in America as they had in the old country, simply appropriated the groundhog ("grundsow" in their language, though I prefer the old Appalachian term I heard growing up, "whistle pig"), which was about that season waking up from hibernation, as the best replacement available. Thus if the groundhog saw its shadow and ducked back into its hole... well, you know the rest. And so we have our contemporary holiday, still celebrated with more enthusiasm among the children of "Dutch" immigrants, especially around eastern Pennsylvania, than anywhere else.

How much, and how many, of our holidays do we acknowledge, knowing down deep that we can't, and shouldn't, take seriously most of what is claimed about them? Maybe the weight of our genes and genetics, along with longstanding custom, is enough to keep holidays alive, though renamed and reworked for meaning, all the way from the days of our ancient nature-worshiping pagan ancestors to modern times. Though I have a mild interest in the prediction of the country's most famous groundhog, Pennsylvania's Punxsutawney Phil, from year to year, I can pretty much take the day or leave it. That said, though, I celebrate my own private holiday in February, one I wish I were able to share fully with my friends and neighbors. I doubt I'll ever be able to do that, however.

I've mentioned that my mother's father lived in our house when I was growing up. His eyesight was terribly poor even at the time I was born, and though he gave me me a great deal of good advice both about school work and chicken raising, probably by the time I was eight years old he was completely blind. But I will never forget what he always found occasion to say in the month of February, even after his eyesight was gone: from the time of his earliest memories until the last, eighty-eighth, year of his life, he'd never seen a February pass without at least one evening of hearing the tree frogs, or spring peepers, sing. And so on that one first, in some years only, warm February day—no matter how cold a winter had been, he'd say, February always managed to borrow a bit from March—he'd sit on our front porch with me, enjoying the peep and chatter of the little tree frogs down along the creek bank and all through the trees around us. Let March 20 or 21 be the first day of spring, let the groundhog be right or wrong: for me, the tree-frog music of that February dusk, sitting in the porch swing with an old man I loved deeply, for me was the true marker of a new spring.

Rest in peace, Grandpa. A day never goes by without me thinking of something you taught me. The music of the tree frogs that I first shared alongside you lives on for another year, and one more renewal of life.

THAT OLD-TIME RELIGION

Not long ago I told you about "A Forgotten Anniversary," the most infamous journalistic hoax of its day. This week I'd like to feature a genuine forgotten anniversary, with no hoax: the month, 137 years ago, that what's now commonly called "Old-Time Religion" came to our section of Appalachia and has remained ever since. This isn't to say that our ancestors didn't worship prior to that time. They certainly did, intently. But before 1880 there was an entire vocabulary of religious terms, now so common across the Bible Belt that many people think of them as having been established by the very Apostles, but which then hadn't even been heard in Kentucky, much less quoted. George Owen Barnes, the so-called Mountain Evangelist, changed all that, and we've not been the same since.

Barnes was a Kentuckian himself, from Stanford in Lincoln County south of Lexington and until 1872, a Presbyterian minister. But during his travels after leaving his denomination he spent time in Chicago and fell in with Dwight Lyman Moody, founder of the Moody Bible Institute. Moody himself had made a prior evangelistic trip to Great Britain and been heavily influenced by an obscure British sect called the Plymouth Brethren, which used a unique form of Bible interpretation and religious terminology and which Moody brought back to America with him. He adopted and used the terms "Great Tribulation" (in capitals), "Rapture" (likewise capitalized, along with its three variants, "Pre-Tribulation," "Mid-Tribulation," and "Post-Tribulation," the latter word often shortened to "Trib"), "Great White Throne Judgment" (as opposed to "the Judgment Seat of Christ," whatever either may mean), and "the plan of salvation" and "personal Savior" in addition to commandeering the sect's "Seven Dispensation" view of humanity. Thus armed, Moody attempted to evangelize the entire country anew. The dogma pretty much requires shaking out the Bible's text as if the individual verses were pieces of a jigsaw puzzle and then trying to wedge them back together to accommodate the doctrines, but it remains integral to modern evangelicalism though it often requires the interpretations of D. L. Moody himself and the Bible commentators and publishers Cyrus Scofield and Charles Ryrie to make any sense. Anyway: after Barnes embraced Moody's positions he secured financial backing from John G. Owsley, a fellow Lincoln Countian who'd struck it rich in Chicago, and back to Kentucky he went to preach Moody's gospel.

Barnes and his evangelistic crew began exhorting in Lexington in late 1879, slowly traveled eastward, and finally reached the Big

Sandy Valley in early February 1880. A hurricane could hardly have caused more tumult. Up and down Levisa Fork the Barnes troupe went that month, staging faith-healing as well as soul-saving, making converts by the hundreds, and even winning support from local ministers. Barnes even managed to found the Pike County community of Elkhorn City, which he originally called "Camp Praise-the-Lord" but which was shortened to "Praise" before the coal companies co-opted the land. He thus introduced Pentecostalism and so-called Holiness to eastern Kentucky even before those movements had adopted formal names, making the area ripe for the proselytizing of the Anderson, Indiana and Cleveland, Tennessee variants of the Church of God, both of which were organized only a few years after Barnes left Kentucky, as well as later and smaller denominations and independent Pentecostal and Holiness churches.

Sadly, Barnes didn't keep a good reputation within the evangelical community. At least his errors were of poor judgment rather than malicious intent. Soon after the big Kentucky revival Barnes and his family joined up with John Alexander Dowie, the self-proclaimed "Prophet Elijah" and founder of the so-called Christian Catholic Apostolic Church. Besides opposing all forms of medical treatment in favor of faith healing, Dowie preached that the earth was both flat and at the center of the universe, and he dressed himself in a bizarre getup based on the biblical description of Aaron's priestly garments in Exodus. About three years before Barnes' death in 1908, Dowie was deposed from leadership in his church for financial impropriety and another charismatic preacher replaced him. Barnes outlived Dowie, but it's likely that the Mountain Evangelist died still believing in "the Prophet's" flat, universe-centered earth and that all medical treatments besides faith healing were sinful.

George Owen Barnes' eastern Kentucky crusade was probably the high point of his ministry. The belief system of our area certainly changed dramatically because of it. But Barnes' story likewise makes it obvious that it's still better to read Scripture through our own eyes rather than his and the sources that he depended on—and come to our own conclusions, wherever reason may lead us.

WHEN LOVE CONQUERED ALL... OR AT LEAST SOMETHING

Anybody that reads my column knows that I enjoy telling tales from work, though confidentiality issues make me be cautious what I relate. But I have another reason for caution, because to be honest, my job is distasteful. I deal regularly—no pun intended—with several messy, malodorous substances that, though we all share them biologically, nobody really cares to talk about except those of us who have had to work with them so much that we've lost our squeamishness. Only the strong of stomach would be brave enough to sit down to a meal with a bunch of Med Techs talking about their professional experiences, and before I learned better I could make everybody around a Sunday dinner table put down their flatware and either leave the table or glare at me, simply because I'd answered the question: "So, John, what did you do this week?"

Anyway, Valentine's Day always makes me recall an incident on the job that could have been tragic but instead kept itself pretty much within the parameters of comedy. There's often a fine line between the two extremes, and I just hope the aftermath went as well. Early in a year more than three decades ago I was called to the Emergency Room to draw a blood alcohol level on one combatant in a fight, a female who had tussled with her boyfriend or spouse and was sporting a sizable pump knot on her head. I'm not sure how badly the male had fared, or in fact if he was even conscious, but when I entered the Emergency Room the woman was in the process of giving the doctor on duty some of the most evocative and sincere blue-hot profanity I have ever heard. I was young and intimidated—this was even before I first met Chuck Q. Farley—but I had a job to do and so when the physician emerged from behind the curtain with a disgusted look and a head shake

I rode into the breach, ready to be cussed altogether as viciously as the doctor had been.

Long story short, for some reason, perhaps because she was so inebriated, the woman thought I was handsome. She never said one ill word to me when I introduced myself, and seemed perfectly willing to cooperate when I asked to draw a sample of her blood. So far, so good, but as I bent down and began to search for a vein in the bend of her right arm something began to crawl upward through my hair, too big for cooties. It was her free hand. She was running the fingers of her left hand through my hair, and evidently enjoying it greatly. I was disquieted, to say the least, but I kept trying to remind myself: female nurses have to put up with this kind of crap not only from male drunks, but some sober guys as well. If they have to deal with it, I guess I can too since it's likely this is the only time it'll ever happen to me. But my patient was by no means done yet. With both of us hidden behind a bed curtain and half a dozen nurses plus the ER doctor outside listening in, she began to moan.

"Oh, baby, baby, baby, PLEASE don't hurt me, babyyyy," she cooed over and over again, interspersing the plea with additional little incoherent squeals as I kept trying to find that durned vein under possibly the most difficult circumstances I have ever attempted a venipuncture. The scalp treatment and the moaning were bad enough on their own, and things only got worse as the ER staff began to listen in as well, and laugh in response to the sounds. Finally my nervous hands managed to draw just enough blood for the test. I withdrew the needle, applied a gauze prep, and raised my head—just as she lifted hers off the gurney, aiming for a kiss. I turned my head and she caught me on the left jaw, right in the beard. My eyes must have bucked like a deer in the headlights. "Stop!" I begged. "You tryin' to lose me my job, or what?" I scooped up my supplies and fled the place like a scalded cat, to the catcalls and applause of my ER coworkers.

Since that freaky little incident I've learned that the bizarre and crazy are simply parts of life, especially hospital life. Every February 14, though,

I think about it—and wonder what further craziness might occur before the year ends. All things considered, just stay tuned.

MY BAPTISM UNDER FIRE

Believe it or not, after Sweet Tater read my Valentine's Day story she actually suggested the topic for today's column. This, even though my recounting of it and similar tales have made so many of her family get up and leave the dinner table only moments after they'd asked me what I'd done the past week. But I suppose it's an occasion every healthcare worker remembers: my personal baptism under fire, that is to say, the very first time I was ever… well, regurgitated upon. So today I'll defer to Sweet Tater's judgment, and bring the story back from recollection's vaults.

It happened in the early eighties, after the May primaries one year because the county in which I was working had not long before "gone wet." A small honky-tonk had gone into business a couple of miles down the road, allowing people who lived in the community—and several from many miles outside it—to indulge publicly in all the excesses they had enjoyed in private during the county's "dry" days. I won't recount the place's name, but it sounded something suspiciously close to the title of a bordello. But at any rate, a bunch of young nurses enjoying a weekend off decided to go a-honky-tonkin' at the dive, and on that circumstance hung the entire chain of events that ultimately led to me. Apparently they found a drunk in the place's parking lot that had fallen face-down in the gravel and possibly aspirated her gastric contents, and they themselves were buzzed enough to think it'd be just a wonderful frolic to load her up in their car and transport her to the hospital as a "Code Blue."

    I first heard about the incoming Code by a phone call from the ER, and initially I thought everything was deadly serious. But at that time, the hospital I worked in was being remodeled, so all ER traffic had to come directly by my workplace and I actually became aware of the patient's arrival before most of the ER staff did. The drunken nurses' attempts to unload the patient and put her on a gurney sounded, literally, like a bunch of giggling teenagers trying to "trim" a shoat (let them that readeth understand that'n), and the pig was justifiably complaining about the entire deal. I shook my head, grabbed my tray, and followed the parade down the hall. One could almost get a secondary high on the alcohol fumes, but that's eastern Kentucky for you. Too many people drink, not to enjoy the taste of a beverage, but to get as drunk as they can as fast as they can.

The sober, on-duty ER caregivers took over as the happy young lovelies tittered and traipsed back out to their car to find more fun somewhere else, and since there weren't enough nurses on duty to immobilize the patient and administer suction at the same time, guess who, with a strong back and a weak mind, got stuck with holding her down. The patient, whose eyes rolled wildly and whose arms were covered from shoulders to wrists with those old homemade do-it-yourself stickpin-and-shoe-polish tattoos so many people used to sport, was simultaneously fighting everyone close enough to slap, and trying to bat the suction apparatus away from her mouth so she could achieve the same result by running her own fingers down her throat.

"Here, John," the senior nurse on duty, who was probably just as irked at her younger colleagues as I was, commanded. "Hold this bedpan close to her face while I turn up the vacuum on the suction." I complied, stepping closer and grabbing the pan as she attended to the valve. All it took was that split second.

The patient never even hit the bedpan. The substance in question flew right across it in a deadly arc. At that moment I was baptized and confirmed as a True Veteran Healthcare Worker.

And so our dramatic liquor-inspired Code Blue was successful. By the time I'd run to the lab, wadded up my stinking, soiled white coat, hurled it into a corner and stalked back to the ER, the patient had evidently gotten rid of everything that was bothering her and was signing herself out against medical advice. I don't recall ever seeing her again after that, so maybe that crazy, haywire excuse for an emergency put her on the strait and narrow. The honky-tonk finally closed down, and we've all grown up a little since then, even those hard-partying young nurses. But there are certain events you just don't forget and, unfortunately, for me this is one of them.

FAN MAIL

Sorry I'm a bit off my game today, but I spent late last night and early this morning trying to calm down Chuck Q. Farley. He rushed to my house past midnight in a panic because... well, just listen in on our conversation.

"Drackler!" he shouted as he banged on my door, "the President's done found out what I said about him back at New Year's and he's mad at me! I got a letter back from him! He hates me!"

I let him in as soon as I recognized his voice, and I tried to comfort him as I scanned the note. "Aw, Chuck Q., there's no need to worry," I said. "You seen any Secret Service people around?"

"If they air, they're hid good," he responded, glancing around nervously.

"Well, the return address on this is 1600 Pennsylvania Avenue, Washington, sure enough, but the postmark's local to here. I don't think the President writes with any pen name like 'Buck Q. Fuddy' the way this person does. He'd rather Tweet. Besides, the letter and envelope are written in pencil! I'm jealous, though. I've not gotten one letter of fan mail yet, and here's your first." I clapped his shoulder and grinned at him.

He blinked. "*FAN* mail? Can't you see how bad he's a-tryin' to make me feel?"

"How can you tell it's a he? Somebody, male or female, just made up this name as a play on yours to hide his—or her—own. This isn't from the President. Likely it's just somebody around here that's been encouraged to be rude by his way of talking on Tweets and in speeches and who's trying to mimic him for some reason."

Chuck Q. shook his head. "Ever' word he can think up to try and make me feel about two inches tall," he sighed. "Castin' all them aspirations on me! All them stupid names! Just because he thinks I don't agree with what he believes. Or she, I know. But you coulda warned me about the risk of such as this," he added with a reproachful look at me.

"Well, Chuck Q., newspapers feel like no publicity is bad publicity. They'll let almost anything go in an opinion piece as long as it doesn't violate State and Federal law. And personally, I think your ideas about the makeup and undertakers weren't half bad. Maybe it's just the way you—and I—stated 'em. But this," I continued, re-scanning the letter, "the most charitable way I can look at it is the writer could be tryin' to sound like a drill instructor. A drill instructor always worries that his recruits might go to battle after basic training and get killed because he didn't teach them how to do something right. So these harsh words, even in the best light they could have been spoken, are based on fear and insecurity, drill instructor or not."

"How you figure?" he asked.

"Unless two people completely lose their tempers and start calling each other names out of rage, any time an adult uses this kind of demeaning talk to another adult it means that the first adult is trying to cover up a mighty powerful insecurity. I think that's why so many people around here put such hope in the President. Times are changing and they're insecure and scared. They're religious, but their faith seems to have gotten just like that song about the Vietnam vet: 'One minute I'd kneel down and pray and the next I'd stand and curse.' Anyhow, hearing the President talk smack like that makes them feel good about themselves somehow, and so they ape him."

"Well, I like the way the President talks, myself!"

"Sure, till this letter came and you got talked to that way yourself. When the shoe's on the other foot it's different. Try to forget this stupid thing, but if you can't help thinking about all the mean names the writer called you, just keep in mind how many nights a week he—or she—may be lying awake till dawn dreading something. Or maybe dreading nothing, which is actually scarier."

Chuck Q. looked at me. "Awful preacherly talk for somebody that ain't preachin' no more," he grumbled. "You sure you shouldn't go back at it?"

"Chuck Q., I think the 'Prosperity Gospel' is hogwash, and I've seen too much out of too many people ever to believe 'Name It and Claim It' again. No way for me to succeed, feeling like that. But don't worry. We'll just try to survive whatever comes, I guess like cockroaches and Keith Richards always manage to do."

BITTER TWITTER & CRUEL DUELS

I miss Chuck Q. Farley this week. He comprehends this sort of thing quicker than I do, but he's still spooked from that mail last week, and afraid to participate so soon in another column. So I guess I've just got to wing it. Trouble is, when I start looking for sense in things sometimes I have a lot of difficulty finding it—particularly all the contemporary hubbub about the President's messages on Twitter. For at least the first half of our country's history, back when Americans were all properly religious and things were supposed generally to be better all around, no self-respecting politician would have considered the equivalent of a modern-day Tweet to be the end of a dispute—rather, merely the beginning. You see, in those days the so-called code duello was still legal in Southern states.

The historic equivalent of an aggressive Tweet—which back then could only have been publicized as a paid newspaper ad or on a handbill—would have been considered merely as a "posting" to provoke an adversary to a duel, also known as an affair of honor, with swords or smooth-bore single-shot pistols. A man thus denounced was expected to issue a challenge to the "poster" in order to avenge his impugned honor, or else be labeled a coward. Then the posting offender was given the choice of weapons, both parties chose "seconds" or assistants, the duel was set up, and unless the seconds could talk the principals out of the whole business or either or both parties missed or fired into the air, the conclusion of the entire mess was somebody's wounding or death. Thomas Jefferson's first Vice President, Aaron Burr, settled things this way with Treasury Secretary Alexander Hamilton over, among other issues, Burr's suspicious relationship with a foreign government (Holland back then, not Russia, but Spain later in Burr's life). Andrew Jackson fought in more than a hundred duels and was said to have kept thirty-seven smooth-bore pistols at the ready in case he should need them. His varied contests ranged from the actual killing of one man, Charles Dickenson, in 1806, to his serving as second to a fellow duelist who shot some poor guy right in the seat of the pants a few years later. And a good many of Kentucky's best-known statesmen, including Henry Clay, Richard Menefee, and William Goebel, were no strangers to the field of honor, if thus it can truly be called, either.

Perhaps the most famous Kentuckian ever challenged to a duel, however, was ashamed of the episode ever afterward. A youthful prairie lawyer named Abraham Lincoln initiated the quarrel through a series of juvenile, sophomoric editorial letters (not unlike modern-day Tweets, just more than 140 characters long) that he composed along with a young Lexington-born lady then known as Mary Todd against Whig politician James Shields. When challenged by Shields and asked his choice of weapon, Lincoln picked the biggest cavalry sabers he could find, figuring perhaps correctly that Shields could outshoot him and knowing that his height gave him the advantage in a swordfight with his smaller adversary. But the two duelists allowed themselves to be talked out of the contest by their seconds and other bystanders, ostensibly salvaging the honor of both, and during his term as President, when Lincoln was asked by an Army officer if it were true that he had once participated in a duel he replied, "I do not deny it, but if you desire my friendship you will never mention it again." Oh, well. What must one expect from these big-Federal-Government liberal types, after all, who tyrannically managed to ram the outlawing of dueling, and so many other practices equally time-

and tradition-honored and pleasant, through the legislatures of every state that had once approved of them?...

But if the Courts would only reconsider the matter, dueling just might once again prove useful in both State and Federal politics. It certainly has the potential. For one thing, the code duello's revival would definitely improve folks' manners on Twitter, and maybe Facebook too. It couldn't hurt to hope that politeness might return to political discourse as well, though the renewed courtesies would be pretty much like those of Huck Finn's father, reformable only by a shotgun. The firearms industry, robbed by the change in Presidential administrations of its chief advertising gimmick, the threat of Government confiscation of firearms, could prosper once again by crafting elegant dueling pistols. And best of all, the practice could prove to be a *GREAT* solution to the problem of term limits. Petition your Congressman today! Or challenge him...

IN DEFENSE OF BEN

I consider myself a liberal about some things and a moderate about others, but although I've been conservative in my time I doubt that anybody would mistake me for one now. Still, I like to think that I can appreciate any proposition across the spectrum so long as it's supported by logic, reason, and historical examples. Thus I have to admit to being in a quandary about Dr. Ben Carson right now. He's a talented neurosurgeon, but about as qualified to lead the Department of Housing and Urban Development as Grizzly Bear Betsy DeVos is equipped to run the Department of Education. That, in itself, is no slur on the man personally. Just because you're good at one or two things doesn't mean you can be master of all trades. Sir Isaac Newton's work revolutionized the study of physics, but he wrote theological works so off-the-wall that neither Churchmen nor freethinkers could approve of them. Similarly Jonathan Edwards, one of the greatest philosophical writers this continent has ever produced, penned the horrible sermon "Sinners in the Hands of an Angry God" and harbored ideas about Bible prophecy that were as bat-dropping crazy as anything you hear from television evangelists right now. Edwards hypothesized that the world would end in 1866, which probably seemed like good sense during the worst days of the Civil War.

Oh, well. Back to the present. Ben Carson has indeed mouthed some egregious nonsense, but I can't help thinking that his latest controversial comment—allegedly equating slaves brought to America in chains during the seventeenth and eighteenth centuries to voluntary immigrants—has been completely misconstrued by those with axes to grind and looking for any chance to find fault with him. True, Carson's choice of words was extremely poor. But I've listened to his speech and read the transcript of it too, and to me the passage in question comes off as a bitterly ironic remark that he spoke tongue-in-cheek, nothing more. I'd tell him he should have chosen his words more carefully, and move on. But no: now he's being vilified by both black and liberal white pundits not only as a poor speaker, but as some sort of traitor to his own people. I think this is such a personal issue with me because I've had my own words twisted so many, many times in my growing-up years, with the absolute worst possible construct applied to them. Few things seem to me to be more unfair, even for politicians.

Now, having your words played with isn't always unpleasant, or even wrong. One of my more vivid youthful memories is of hoeing the garden with Dad, whom I'd outdistanced in a race to the ends of our respective rows, and commenting, "I guess this shows that I'm a good hoer." No one who knew my father would expect him to ignore a thoughtless remark like that—and he didn't. I turned beet-red at his reply, but I simply had to take his laughter in stride: open mouth, insert foot.

Not so with another relative, whose identity I won't divulge. With a bone-deep victim mentality I didn't even realize existed until years later, this individual could and did twist the most innocent, innocuous remarks into personal attacks worthy of furious responses that lasted anywhere from hours to weeks—a tendency that the relative seldom if ever revealed to anyone outside the family. The mood simply and abruptly changed with the arrival of visitors and then returned like a summer thunderhead when they left, often with criticisms of the visitors added to the original complaint. Talk about putting the "func" in "dysfunctional!" But that's the reason I bristle when I hear somebody's words being twisted purposefully and disproportionately, even if I completely disagree with the individual being quoted. I've been there, had that done, and still quill up like a porcupine and back into a corner if I sense it's happening to me again.

But I'm a survivor, not a victim, and so I try to focus on the more lighthearted things I've seen, like the old preacher so aggrieved about women keeping wigs at home in their bureau drawers that he proclaimed during a sermon that "women these days got more hair in their drawers than they do on their heads!" (True story.) If you thought about what he said you could discern what he meant, but that didn't stop the entire congregation that Sunday from completely breaking up laughing. All too seldom, though, is a misconstruction funny. My advice: ease up on Carson and save your outrage for the genuine dangers we have going right now.

ANOTHER MODEST PROPOSAL

Chuck Q. Farley's cheered back up after his fan mail scare, but now he's working on ways to impress the President just in case. His latest scheme's a prime example, and although I don't have the heart to tell him neither the President nor Congress will ever consider the idea, let alone pass it as a bill, I'll be dogged if it doesn't actually sound reasonable. You decide. Our most recent phone conversation went something like this:

"Drackler! I've come up with the perfect idear to get the President to like me again! That is, if it WAS him who wrote me that fan letter. If not, I bet he'll still approve the notion! You know that

Johnson Amendment thing that won't let the churches have their Freedom of Speech?"

"Well, the Johnson Amendment's not that simple, Chuck Q. It forbids non-profit organizations like churches from making political endorsements if they want to keep their tax-exempt status. If they campaign they've got to pay their taxes. It's named for Lyndon Johnson, from the days when he was a Senator. He led the measure through Congress back in 1954 so President Eisenhower could sign it into law. Johnson was a Democrat, Eisenhower a Republican, but they worked together to get that law passed and it's a good one.

"But I didn't think people around here paid much attention to it anyway. My folks used to talk about how churches around here campaigned against John F. Kennedy in 1960, six years after the Amendment became law, because he was Catholic, and this past November right before the election I heard a preacher on the radio locally tell his listeners which candidate had his vote. Although he never actually told his listeners who they should vote for, his implication was about as subtle as a sledgehammer. I guess he thought somebody wanted him to remind us."

"Well, then," retorted Chuck Q. in a puzzled voice, "I wonder what's the big deal! Anyhow, I know for a fact the President's agin' the thing because he said so on TV, and I've figgered a way so's he don't have to fight nor Tweet no more judges nor liberals nor Democrats nor any of them other ungodly heatherns keepin' him from doin' the Lord's work."

I asked Chuck Q. to hold while I popped a couple of aspirin, but my curiosity got the better of my headache so I picked the phone back up. "All, right, Chuck Q.," I encouraged him, "tell me more."

"Drackler, it's plumb simple," he replied happily. "All the churches got to do is start payin' their taxes, and then they can tell their people who to vote for with complete Freedom of Speech!"

I was tempted to pop a third aspirin, but the more I thought about his plan the less I could see wrong with it. Loads of tax money goes to feed and aid the poor—and if those programs aren't 100% perfect, I'd seen few churches, especially those stressing tithing, act too wisely with their own money either. From what I'd seen, they often spent a great deal of it on carpet and PA systems and decorations and such, and even if their treasurers were trustworthy (not always the case—I'd known a few who swore that "God knows my heart!" even as they embezzled money) sometimes it just disappeared anyway, no questions asked. Tuition can be surprisingly steep when you get your theological training in the School of Experience.

But all things considered, why shouldn't the churches pay taxes? At least a little of the cash they raked in might actually make it to social programs where it would do some good. The Government couldn't waste it any worse than a lot of them managed to accomplish themselves. And too, that way they'd have all the political voice they wanted without ever violating the Johnson Amendment. Ultimately I had to agree with Chuck Q.'s plan and I told him so.

"Well, Drackler, one more thing," he concluded. "You bein' a ex-preacher, do you still remember some Bible that'd back my idear up?"

"Sure," I answered. "Start with Matthew 17:24-27, go from there to chapter 22: 16-21 in the same book, and wind up with Romans 13:6-8."

"Thanks, Drackler, you're a true friend!" he enthused. "I'll write the President today, and some pastors too. And I can look forward to gettin' fan mail for this one, because the Lord's people all love one another!"

"Well, I hope so, Chuck Q.," I replied, "but like John Collier ended that famous short story of his: *'au revoir.'*"

LIONS, LAMBS, & LOVIN'

It's almost April now, and no doubt you've heard the old adage that "if March comes in like a lion it'll go out like a lamb," and its corollary reversing the roles of lamb and lion, at least once or twice already. We got rain on March 1 this year, so I guess that qualifies as lionish weather. It's a folk tradition that, as far as I can learn, has no real basis in any ancient holiday, but the saying itself seems almost as old as the hills. A bunch of questionable Internet sources call it an "eighteenth century saw," and one Wikipedia article claims it originated, like the role of the groundhog for February 2, in Pennsylvania. Some astrologers think of it in terms of the Zodiac: Leo the Lion is said to be the rising sign at sunset in early March, giving way to Aries the Ram later on in the month, though a full-grown ram's a far cry from a little lamb. A few mystics interpret it as Jesus coming first as a sacrificial lamb but in the future as the Lion of the Tribe of Judah, although that claim doesn't quite explain what happens if the lion comes at the first of the month and the lamb at the last. In short, nobody—and I mean *NOBODY*—agrees on where this old proverb got its start.

Perhaps the whole idea simply has to do with the sense of balance that we humans seem always to have harbored and maintained. As the third chapter of Ecclesiastes tells us, there's a time for every purpose under heaven and a season for all things, including hot and cold, sowing and reaping, living and dying, war and peace. That's about the only thing you ever hear quoted around here from Ecclesiastes besides a couple of verses I can think of in its final chapter, but there's a great deal of wisdom throughout the text that's readily available with little or no looking—if it's really wisdom you're seeking, rather than backup for an opinion you've already determined to maintain come what may. Or maybe the origins of the March expression are simply lost to us in the fog of the days before humankind developed writing, and its beginnings are literally anybody's guess. I recall years when it came true for both the first and last of the month of March, and years when it didn't. But I remember one early spring, thirty years ago at this writing, that the season actually added another critter to the mix of lion and lamb, one which nobody quite expected at first and which didn't really manifest itself until some months later. And like Bret Harte once had his character Truthful James say, the same I would rise to explain.

The so-called Spring Blizzard of 1987 actually waited until after the end of March to blow in, occurring between April 2 and April 5 with three or four days of cleanup following. By Friday, April 3, almost all eastern Kentucky was paralyzed, and many of us healthcare folk had to spend the entire weekend working long shifts because there was no way to get out of our hospitals and no place to go even if we could. Sweet Tater and I had only one Tater Tot at the time and all I could do was telephone them to say that I missed them and I hoped all the ice didn't snap the phone lines. Dad was sick then, too, adding to my worries. But like most else I've had thrown at me over the years, I weathered out the blizzard and finally got home in time to spend a couple days off swinging a snow shovel. Now, shoveling deep, wet snow is tough, but it was still nothing like the effort I had to expend in the lab thirty-seven to forty weeks later, when it seemed that every young mother in three or four counties chose that particular time for a certain labor all their own.

Yep. That's right. In January 1988 our hospital hosted the largest number of baby deliveries I ever recall seeing at one time. Most, if not all, had to have been conceived during the Spring Blizzard. I guess the young married couples of the Big Sandy Valley had to think up some way to combat boredom during the snowstorm. Everybody needs a hobby, after all. But if March went out like a lion that year there must have been a rabbit somewhere in the mix as well, and the little varmint definitely outran the big one.

MY GOD!

The other day a well-dressed fellow carrying an ornate Ryrie Study Bible accosted me in the parking lot of a local supermarket. He introduced himself and inquired, "Mr. Tater, I presume?"

"Just call me Common," I answered, shaking his hand.

"Very well, then, uh… Common, I wanted to speak with you because the overall tone of your writing, especially your recent column addressing the issue of church taxing, leads me to think you're lost and need to find Jesus."

Strictly speaking, that idea about church taxing was Chuck Q. Farley's, but since Chuck Q. got such a fright recently I was glad to take the rap for him. "With all due respect, sir, I deny the allegation and dispute the allegator," I replied. "I live near the mouth of Burnt Cabin and I know exactly which roads to take to get home. I'm not lost, and as for finding Jesus, I didn't think he was lost either."

A nostril flared briefly, but his smile stayed intact. "My friend," he persisted, "you obviously need to meet my God. Now my Bible tells me that my God—"

"YOUR Bible and YOUR God?"

"Yes! My Bible and my God! They should be yours, too!"

"Who wrote your Bible? That guy Ryrie whose name's on the cover? Or was it Scofield or maybe Thompson instead?"

The smile faded and he glared at me like a teacher dealing with a disrespectful schoolboy. "My God wrote this book!" he thundered at me, holding the volume upright as if it were a weapon or shield. "He wrote it through special men inspired by the Holy Spirit, and it's all true, cover to cover, without one single word of error in it! Charles Ryrie and Cyrus Scofield and Frank Thompson were merely godly scholars who had some good ideas about it and wrote commentaries at the sides of the text and in the footnotes!"

"I see. Well, if that's the case, would you read Job 2:3 to me, please?"

He frowned, but opened the Bible, found the verse and complied. He read slowly too, which I'd hoped he would so he'd get every nuance of meaning out of it, from the good old King James Version:

"'And the Lord said unto Satan, Hast thou considered my servant Job, that there is none like him in the earth, a perfect and upright man, one that feareth God, and escheweth evil? And still he holdeth fast his integrity, although thou…

movedest me against him, to… destroy… him… without… cause…'"

His voice trailed off but his eyes flashed fire. "Now you wait just a minute!" he barked with all the authority he could muster, shaking the open book at me. "My Bible tells me that my God don't do NOTHIN' without a just and righteous cause! How dare you imply otherwise?"

"I only asked you to read a verse," I countered mildly. "I'd hoped you'd tell me who went to heaven to hear God say that to Satan and then returned to earth to write it down. But you bring up another good point. God said right there in your Bible that he destroyed Job without cause, and the only reason he gave was that Satan 'moved' him to do so. God's own words, nobody else's, and it's the same in EVERY translation, not just the King James. And if that's true and inerrant, it begs some tough questions."

"Atheist! Muslin! Infidel! Scripture-quotin' devil!" he bleated, stepping back with an alarmed look and holding his book between himself and me, maybe for protection. "'O full of all subtility and all mischief, thou child of the devil, thou enemy of all righteousness, wilt thou not cease to pervert the right ways of the Lord?'"

"Acts 13:10," I said softly as he blinked his eyes. "You can throw verse 11 at me too if you like. But 'muslin' is a fabric, and say whatever else you will about me, I'm no longer a man of the cloth. Nowadays I just try my best to encourage people to think, period—and not to be scared that God's gonna send 'em to hell for doing it. So why don't I offer you a blessing in exchange for your curse, and we call it even?"

"What do you mean?" he muttered, still scowling suspiciously.

I laid my left hand on his right shoulder, raised my right hand high in the air, bowed my head, and intoned, "May the God of your choice bless you. Ay-MAY-un."

"Uh… thank you," he responded, turning to leave.

"You're entirely welcome," I answered as I opened my truck door.

THE EVOLUTION OF FRIENDSHIP

"Drackler, looks like you got more response to my church tax idear than I did," said Chuck Q. Farley to me this past weekend as we were fishing. He sounded a bit jealous, but after the conversation I'd endured the week before in town, I'd have been glad to switch places with him.

"But I ain't discouraged yet," he continued. "I've got me another idear that anybody religious ort to get behind a hundred and one percent."

"And I'll publicize it for you in Tater Text, right?" I winked at him.

"Shore. Who else is gon' give you stuff to write about besides me and Polly Esther?"

"Point taken," I admitted, casting my line. "Sweet Tater won't let me write about her. Shoot."

"Well, it's this evolution thing in the schools. They's just somethin' about protestin' it that don't make no sense to me and I wisht I knowed why folks think how they do."

"Me too," I replied. "When I used to pastor, during any church trouble I was always glad when I could keep a congregation FROM acting like a bunch of monkeys. 'Specially over in the next county, though goodness knows this one's bad enough. Ask any pastor in private and he'll tell you the same, no matter what he says in public about either creation or his flock. But I'm warning you: evolution is such a touchy subject around here you'll find very few people who'll talk about it reasonably. A lot of 'em figure if they show any support for the idea at all, their friends and neighbors'll think they're heathens or something. You know how eastern Kentucky is."

"Well, I can fix that," continued Chuck Q. "Ever'thing'd line up if people would only follow Ecclesiastes, first chapter, fifth verse. I got it memorized too! 'The sun also ariseth, and the sun goeth down, and hasteth to his place where he arose.'"

I looked at him and arched an eyebrow. "I'm familiar with that one," I answered. "Ernest Hemingway used part of it for a book title, and then one well-known sect bases a lot of its doctrine on the verse right before it, where it reads 'the earth abideth forever.' But what's the 'sun also ariseth' verse got to do with evolution?"

"Why, Drackler, can't you see? The earth don't go around the sun, the sun goes around the earth! Bible says so plain right there. And they's other verses backs that up too. So I figure as long as they're teachin' our children that the earth goes around the sun instead of what the Bible plainly says happens, they can't fight evolution because they're bypassin' the very foundation of creation. I aim to start up a crusade for teachers to teach about the earth and sun the right way. THEN they can fix evolution."

I cast my line again and pondered. "Well," I began, "years ago I knew two old ministers who believed and preached that way, but I've not heard anything similar from the pulpit since their day. And that doesn't even get into the trouble old Galileo caught a few hundred years ago for questioning the idea, or how as late as 1951

Thomas Merton still defended the Church for treating Galileo the way it did. But Chuck Q.—"

I paused to collect my thoughts. Lord, he was so earnest about this! I hated to burst his bubble, but I had to do something to keep my friend from even more turmoil. So I told him the truth.

"Chuck Q., I don't know how else to say it, but—nobody'll listen. You'll only get yourself a troublemaker's reputation. You and I both know what that verse says. But for some reason people want to take the first part of Genesis literally and they don't want to take that verse in Ecclesiastes the same way, and if you start reminding them of the inconsistency that shows, they'll just get mad at you for bringing up the subject and start attacking you personally. It's like the song lyrics: 'Some call it dreamin', then let me dream on.' Most people'd rather die than think anything out for themselves. That's just how humans are. I'm sorry."

Chuck Q. looked sad for a moment. "Well, then, maybe I'm somethin' like—Galileo, huh?" he asked me hopefully.

I clapped him on the shoulder and grinned. "Shucks, why not?" I assured him. "We're all just disciples a-fishin' anyway, and Easter's comin' up next Sunday. Hey, you got a bite! Set your hook! Maybe that fish'll even have tax money in its mouth, like the one in Matthew 17."

NATURALIZED

"Drackler, I've had some fits and starts since I've been helpin' you with your colyum, but I'm gettin' the hang of this political stuff now," said Chuck Q. Farley. He sat on the tailgate of his old pickup near my garden as his and Polly Esther's oldest son, Chuck Q. Farley Two, helped me plant white half-runners. I've mentioned before that Chuck Q., Senior, respects both work and his mother so much that he's never hit either of them a lick in his life, but he doesn't mind watching his son work. Out of respect for it, of course, but regardless, he'll ask me for the son's pay. The setup reminds me of an uncle and cousin of mine, although the cousin wound up killing a law officer and then himself. I hope this boy doesn't turn out that way.

"Well, you're one up on me, then, Chuck Q.," I grumbled, "because it seems to me that things just get crazier every day. Remember what I said right after the election, how the farmers downstate where I work are going to be out of field labor this summer if that wall goes up and Immigration agents keep coming down on Hispanics? And I just don't understand. We get lots of Hispanics in the hospital there, mostly around tobacco-cuttin' time with nicotine poisoning from them luggin' tobacco into hot, stuffy barns on bare backs, but then there's infected cuts from the tobacco stakes besides sick kids all year long. And those people work like dogs, on jobs that white—well, I mean native county people—won't do any more because welfare pays better. Never saw an immigrant family down there that didn't work like a-fightin' fire. Now let's see 'em try to talk who's left and available into workin'." I shook my head.

"Can I catch a ride down there with you?" Chuck Q. Two murmured, glancing at his father.

"Anytime, son, if you'll stick with it," I replied.

"He ain't gon' need to do that," interjected Chuck Q. from the tailgate. "President's gonna have so many mine jobs openin' up he can stay right here. Just wait."

"Well, Chuck Q., you oughta be able to get one yourself then," I retorted, finishing up a furrow.

"*ME?* Drackler, I've done told you and the boy and Polly Esther all, I *RESPECT* work. In fact I respect it so much that—"

"Yeah, yeah. Quick, let's change the subject. Gimme another political idea to write about."

"All right, iffen you feel that way about it," he rejoined, slightly miffed. "Well, then, I was thinkin' about them poor Standin' Rock Sioux that protested the pipeline out west and give the

Government such trouble. I hate to see 'em like that. Now they need work too, so why don't the President just take all the able-bodied Injuns that protested, and give 'em jobs with the I.N.S.? He's gonna need a lot more Immigration agents."

The boy snorted. I wiped sweat from my forehead, leaned on my hoe, and looked at Chuck Q.

"Let me get this straight," I asked him, "you want the President of the United States to give members of an American Indian tribe jobs as agents for the Immigration and Naturalization Service, with the power to arrest and imprison illegal aliens?"

Chuck Q. nodded. "And if it works," he continued, "maybe a big bunch of Injuns in a lot more tribes can get jobs with 'em too. It'd keep 'em from makin' good white folks do all that sinful gamblin' and cavortin' around in all them casinos they've got."

"And since the President's so busy makin' America great right now, should he just give all those brand-new Native American I.N.S. agents authority to deport whomever they think MIGHT be illegal immigrants, too?"

"You got the idear now, Drackler. It'd be a load offen that good man's shoulders."

"Good point. They're supportin' his head already. Chuck Q., I swear I'm gonna run you for political office one day," I told him as I started another furrow. "You're a natural at it."

"Now hold it," he protested, alarmed. "Drackler, I'm tellin' you again, I *RESPECT* work —"

"Shoot, Chuck Q., politicians don't work," I assured him. "All they do is get gullible people to believe stuff, and they use a lot cheaper—and smellier—bait for that than you and I do when we fish."

Sweet Tater came to the porch with a pitcher and a tray of cups. "You all want some water?" she called out.

"We'll break in a minute, honey," I answered, "but just in case—pack us some suitcases, okay?"

THE KENTUCKY TERRORIST

If ever there were two hated words in the United States from the late 1940s to the late 1980s, they were "Communism" and "Communists." Similarly, two of the most-hated words from the mid-1980s to the present are "terrorism" and "terrorists." Neither of the latter is new, though. They both hark all the way back to the French Revolution when they were used to describe Robespierre's government and its agents during the Reign of Terror, certainly one of world history's worst examples of good intentions gone bad. And sadly, there have been terrorists, and acts of terrorism, skulking through American history too, long before the terms were ever revived to recount current events; some, perhaps many, not out-and-out evil people, but maybe simply caught up in the events swirling around them to the point that they began to forget their own humanity. The prime example that comes to mind is Kentucky's twenty-eighth Governor, Luke Pryor Blackburn, who served the state between 1879 and 1883—and the

Confederacy in much more secretive ways, sixteen to twenty years earlier.

Blackburn got his start with both public service and a lifelong interest in infectious diseases while in medical school at Transylvania College during Lexington's terrible cholera epidemic of 1833-34. After receiving his medical degree he was instrumental in combating another outbreak of the dread disease in Versailles the year afterward, later migrating to Natchez, Mississippi and then to New Orleans where he studied yellow fever and eventually established himself as one of the United States' leading authorities on it. He set up quarantines, lobbied for the construction of hospitals, and was called to assist in combating yellow fever outbreaks as far away as New York City in the north and Bermuda in the south. Often he served without pay, and once even founded a hospital for Mississippi riverboat workers using his own personal funds. He appears to have been a genuinely kind and generous man for most of his life, which makes his behavior during the last days of the Civil War all the more confusing and troubling.

Though he was too old to enlist in the Confederate Army, Blackburn served at different times as military surgeon, Confederate medical commissioner, and envoy between Louisiana and Kentucky for weapons exchange and transfer. Then late in the war he somehow got involved in espionage as well, traveling to Canada to collect provisions for blockade-running ships along the Atlantic Coast, and he once even participated in a blockade run himself. He remained in Canada for the rest of the war, and as the Confederacy fell he came up with a plan completely out of character for any physician inclined to keep the Hippocratic Oath, let alone one with such prior dedication to stamping out infectious diseases: he arranged with two other Confederate secret agents to smuggle trunks of clothing and bedding from patients suffering with yellow fever from the Deep South to Northern cities in the hopes of starting large-scale epidemics all across the Union, just like the anthrax mailers after 9/11. One of Blackburn's henchmen even managed to ship a full suitcase to the White House itself. After his postwar return to Kentucky and during his political career, Blackburn always denied involvement in the yellow fever project—but evidence from two independent sources appears to contradict his protestations of innocence.

Blackburn died in peace, and years passed before the military physician Walter Reed discovered that yellow fever was transmitted solely through the bite of the Aedes mosquito and not through direct human contact. Thus the clothing that Blackburn had routed from the Confederacy to the North was comparatively harmless, though no one could have known it at the time. But did Blackburn's lack of knowledge about yellow fever's true etiology provide any excuse for his intent? He acted in a time of desperation for the survival of the Confederacy, and I can't help but wonder what would have happened if he'd picked cholera instead of yellow fever for his germ warfare do-or-die gamble and had succeeded in killing Abraham, Mary, and Tad Lincoln as well as untold thousands of Northerners. Would the Confederacy ultimately have triumphed, and would Blackburn have been hailed as a pioneer scientific military tactician? Would germ warfare have caught on a hundred years before it actually did, and with it, repeated disease attacks between Union and Confederacy until both had eaten one another up? It's almost too uncomfortable even to consider, but worst of all: if Governor Blackburn thus allowed himself to become a terrorist, how little might it take for any of us to act likewise? Sweet dreams over that one.

www.ingramcontent.com/pod-product-compliance
Lightning Source LLC
Chambersburg PA
CBHW030529010526
44110CB00048B/786